Sacraments

and

Shamans

D1016762

Sacraments and Shamans

A Priest Journeys Among Native Peoples

Scott McCarthy

Blue Dolphin Publishing

Copyright © 2011 Scott McCarthy
All rights reserved.

Published by Blue Dolphin Publishing, Inc.
P. O. Box 8, Nevada City, CA 95959
Orders: 1-800-643-0765
Web: www.bluedolphinpublishing.com

ISBN: 978-1-57733-246-6 paperback
ISBN: 978-1-57733-404-0 e-book

Library of Congress Cataloging-in-Publication Data

McCarthy, Scott.
Sacraments and shamans : a priest journeys among native peoples / Scott McCarthy.
p. cm.
ISBN 978-1-57733-246-6 (pbk. : alk. paper)
1. Indians of North America—Religion. 2. Indians of North America—Rites and ceremonies. 3. McCarthy, Scott—Travel—North America. I. Title.
E59.R38M34 2010
299.7—dc22
2010022036

Francis; The Journey and the Dream, copyright 1988, by Murray Bodo, O.F.M., reprinted with permission of St. Anthony Messenger Press, 28 W. Liberty St., Cincinnati, OH 45202

First edition March 2011

Printed in the United States of America

10 9 8 7 6 5 4 3 2 1

Dedication

I DEDICATE THIS WORK to the wonderful people around us all:
those who like to share, discuss realities great and small,
eat and drink, observe and create art, dance, pray,
be kind to animals and plants, and really live
so that others may enjoy life abundantly.
We already know who *some* of them are.
Whatever their cultural context, may their tribes increase!

This dedication also belongs to all those priests, ministers, shamans, and spiritual leaders throughout the world who give their very lives for their people. May they be blessed by God and venerated among their sisters and brothers!

Contents

Acknowledgments xi

Introduction 1

England 4

Early Life 4

Canada 8

The New Land 8

Crossing the Atlantic Sea 9

A Very Different Terrain 11

First Contacts 12

Indiancrafts 14

Iroquois Pageant 15

Canadian History 20

California 24

Another New Home 24

California Tribes 29

Watsonville: Saint Patrick's 31

Life as a Priest 33

Early Years of Priesthood 33

Capitola: Saint Joseph's 34

A Child Is Born 35

A Young Person Enters into Greater Life 36

Santa Cruz: Holy Cross 40

A Spiritual Experience: Vision Questing 42

San Luis Obispo: The Old Mission 45

Chumash Country 46

New Friends 47

Tradition 47

Artichokeland: First Pastorate: Castroville 51

Vacations 55

Visit of Pope John Paul II to Monterey 61

Kateri Circle 63

A Special Guest 65

1989 Earthquake 66

Crow Adoption Preliminaries 67

Lakota Friends 68

New Crow Friends 70

Sabbatical Time 73

Making Plans 73

The Journey Continues 73

An Eagle 74

Activities 74

Sundance Preparations 78

A Little Bit of Paradise: Second Pastorate: Carmel Valley 80

A Unique Sweatlodge 81

Powwows in Prison 85

Priests Serving California Native People 86

American Indian Movement Personalities 87

Grow Ventre Sundance 90

My Book on Native Spirituality:
People of the Circle, People of the Four Directions 91

A Pomo Medicine Woman 93

Bear Dances 95

A Four Directions Ceremony and
a Lake Circling Blessing 97

An Historic Funeral 98

A School Presentation 99

Blessing of Monterey Bay 100

Native Gathering of the Americas 101
Ramiro 106
Gregorio 106
Santiago 108
Martin 110
Carmona Family 111
Santos 112
Ramón 115
Kuala 116
Rubén and Friends 118
Sharman 120
Sights Seen 121
Invitations 121
A Visit to a Shaman 122
Maria Lionza 131
Belize 135
Island of Dominica 137
Panama 141
Costa Rica 150
Brazil 151
Santo Daime 152
Healing a Shaman 155
A Massacre 159
Two Bishops, A Priest, and a Prophet 160
Guyana 168
Colombia 171
More Recently 173
Catholic Digest Magazine 173
An Ocean View: Third Pastorate: Seaside 177
Activities 179
Future Possibilities 183
People Circles 183
Native Island Youth Cultural Exchanges 184

Indigenous Journeys in the Four Directions 186
Spiritual Leadership 187
A Theology of Ecology 194
About the Author 197

Acknowledgments

SO MANY WONDERFUL PEOPLE have helped me to enjoy life and to broaden my vision through travel. Some were in my life for long periods of time, others much less. But each one has profoundly touched me in a special way, each one has somehow connected me with both *the journey and the dream* of my life, and therefore, I am grateful:

Francia Ala (Guatemala), Eileen Alexander, Reverend Joel Almendras, Tim Amaral, Jon and Phyllis Arcuni (Panama), Genaro Arista (Colorado), Gabriel Arreola, Michael Yahureibo Arroyo (Puerto Rico),

Chief David Bald Eagle (South Dakota), Dennis Banks, Edmond Benech, Ron and Toni Bird (Montana), Most Reverend Carlos María Ariz Bolea (Panama), Climaco Bolivar, Shaman Bolivar and Family (Venezuela), Colleen Bonfiglio, Roberto Mucaro Borrero (New York), Reverend Giuseppe Bórtoli (Venezuela), Julicio Browne, Monsignor Michael Buckley *rip*, Rocky Bulltail *rip* (Montana),

Gregorio Cortez Cadales (Venezuela), Rufino Calderon, Calibrato and Climaco (Venezuela), Teresa and Chemo Candelaria Family, Most Reverend Pedro Hernández Cantarero (Panama), Stuart Carlsen, Ernie and Roseangel Carmona Family, Justus Casale, José Castrejón, Alex Castro, Rey Chairez, Pete Chiefchild (Montana), Gina Valdez Chiono, Chiono Family, Chris Christie, Reverend John Clarke (Guyana), Most Reverend Harry Clinch *rip*, Doña Angelbertha Cobb, Santos Cortes, Carlo and Anna Cortopassi, Filip Cunha, Mike Curran,

Most Reverend José Luis Davisson (Venezuela), Jesse de la Cruz, Julio de la Cruz, Frank Delgado, Joe Dominguez, Diane Douglas, Noé Cruz Durán,

Alfredo Escandón (Idaho),

Heike Figueroa, Desray Fox *rip* (Guyana), Chief Hilary Frederick *rip* (Dominica),

Manuel and Marisol Gaitan, Shaman Miguel Gaitan and Family (Venezuela), Ricky Gaitan, Pablo Galaz, Most Reverend Richard García, Allison Gardner, Governor Liborio Garulla (Venezuela), Waeva Gatlin, Robert and Gaby Geisler, Reverend Al Giaquinto, Reverend Dennis Gilbert, Eder Gómez, Lucindo (Kuala) Gómez (Panama), Javier González, José Gonzales, Chief Dwayne Goodface, Reverend Randolph Grayck (Montana), Rabbi Bruce Greenbaum, Nancy Guzmán (Venezuela),

Reverend John Hascall (Michigan), Sharman Haverly, Heath Roberto Hernandez, Jesús Hidalgo, Michael Hoerni *rip,* Patrick Hohmann, Patrick Hohmann, Jeffrey Hopson,

Jahnigen-Krilanovich Family, Fredy Enrique Ortega Jarrin (Costa Rica), Oscar Jauregui, Ed and Sara Johnson (Idaho), Reverend Collins (C.P.) Jordan *rip* (South Dakota), Victor Juarez, Michael June,

Paul Kay, Will Keewatin (Canada), Monsignor John Kennedy *rip,* Reverend Doctor Noel King *rip,* Hermano José María Korta S.J., Richard "Cody" Kostkas, Brian Krilanovich *rip,*

Reverend Joan Laliberty (Idaho), Robert Lamvik, Robert LaRocca, Rubén Lemus, Patrick Leonard, Ramiro Lizaola (Nevada), Obed López (Belize), Aaron López, Alvaro López, José Arturo López, Juan López), Luis López, Robert López, Blaine Lucero *rip* (New Mexico),

Juan Mancias (Texas), Adele and Jonathan Margolis, Justin Marshall, Robert Martin, Calibrato Martinez, Emilio Martinez, Rigoberto Martinez, Ricky Mendoza, Omar Mercado, Louella Merchant (Montana), Dennis and Claudia Meza, Ramiro Millan (Puerto Rico), Elquin Nuñez Miró (Panama), Sister Kateri Mitchell (Montana), Alex Mohr, Ismael Pedroso Moreira (Brazil), Alighieri Morris (Panama), Evaney Morris (Panama), Antonio and Jean Moure (Texas), Martin Muñoz,

Janet McCloud (Washington), Reverend Gerry McCormick, Reverend John McEvoy *rip,* Anne D. McGowan, Reverend George McMenamin *rip,* Reverend Declan Murphy,

Orlando Nakai, Tom Nakai (New Mexico), Tom Nason, Dr. Ramón Nenadich, Reverend Jim Nisbet, Virginia Nobida, Darrell Nomee (Montana),

Santiago Obispo (Venezuela), Ken and Smiley One Feather (South Dakota), Preston and Maria Onion (Montana), Thomas Onion (Montana), Louis Oropeza, Guey Martín Colondres Ortíz and Wakia Arawaka Taina (Puerto Rico), José and Alana Ortiz, Patrick Orozco, Fabián Osornio,

Most Reverend Roque Paloschi (Brazil), Tek Itzép Diego Pasá (Guatemala), Reverend Dan Paul, Gerry Petkus, Paul Peralta, Ralph Perez, Shaman Jose Luís Piaroa and Family (Venezuela), Edward Pio, Bert Plainbull Family (Montana), Gordon and (Phyllis *rip*) Plainbull (Montana), Turk Plainbull (Montana), John Plainfeather *rip* (Montana), Lee Plentywolf (South Dakota), Gay Howard Pollock, Dennis and Jean Powell, Edward Power,

Reverend Oliver Rafferty (Guyana), Samuel Ramos, Victor Rey, Suni Reyna, George Rios, Mary Riotutar Family, Reverend Charles Robinson (Montana), Arnulfo Rocha, George Rocha, Jesús Rocha, Manuel Rocha, Carolyn Rodriguez (Guyana), Hector Rodriguez, José Rodriguez, Juan Rodriguez, Tacho Rodriguez, Daniel Rojas (Costa Rica), Reverend Carlos (Caliche), Ortíz Romero (Colombia), Arturo Rosette, Most Reverend Sylvester Ryan,

Osman Salamanca, Justin Salinas, Gilbert and Nena Sanchez Family, Reverend Max Santamaría (Spain), David and Shinja Scheidnes, Maurice Smith (Belize), Ed and Annemarie Schmitz, The St. Johns *rip* (South Dakota), Ali García Segura (Costa Rica), John and Patricia Kay Shubeck, Most Reverend Thaddeus Shubsda *rip*, Reverend Igór Simonovis (Lithuania), Jill Jurgens Smith, George Solano (Nevada), Jim Starkewolf, Leon Stiffarm (Oregon), Reverend Deborah Streeter, Ervin and Sara Stuart *rip* (Montana),

Janice and Michael Tancredi, Roderick Thomas (Arizona), Bernice Torres *rip*, Albert Tovar, Juan Trejo, Rigoberta Menchú Tum (Guatemala), Eva Tuosto, Jeptha and Esperanza Turner, Jeremy Two Feathers,

John and Jane Upp,

Sue Valdez, Cacique Domingos Savio Veloso Vaz (Brazil), Shaman Raimundo Veloso Vaez (Brazil), Felipe Cruz Vargas, Miguel Vargas, Ricardo Vasquez, Martín Veguilla and Concilio Guata-Ma-Cu a Borikén (Puerto Rico), Robert Virgin, Michael Vizcarra,

Most Reverend José Song Sui Wan (Brazil), John Warren, Sean Warren, Floyd Westerman *rip* (South Dakota), Norman and Angeline Whiteman Family (Montana), Mary Jane Wilson *rip* (Minnesota).

Introduction

HAVE YOU EVER BEEN TO A FARAWAY PLACE like northern Ontario, Canada, or Darién, Panama, or even the Brazilian Amazon and experienced a sunrise or a sunset from a hand-made canoe?

Have you ever imagined yourself walking along a jungle trail to visit the home of a shaman and his extended family?

Have you ever said, "Oh, I can't do that because the jungle is too hot and steamy, because there are too many jaguars and giant spiders and poisonous snakes, and not enough ice cubes and air conditioning readily available"?

Have you surmised that there are no Best Western or Hilton hotels situated close enough to the jungle for your own comfort, and so you just stay home?

Well, I have had similar thoughts. I like my creature comforts, but I also enjoy the call of adventure much more!

Quite often I choose to spend periods of time in unique or even exotic places in order to get acquainted with families living there just to see how they experience daily life.

In my travels through life as well as across the globe, I really appreciate spending time with indigenous People (tribes, ethnic groups, bands, individuals) as well as with mixed heritage folks (*metís, mestizos, criollos*, creoles, "half breeds," *ladinos*, etc.). Usually visiting as a friend, I am not seen as someone on an official mission of some kind. Sometimes shamans and I make important spiritual connections and we soon become fast friends as well as colleagues in spirituality.

As a spiritual leader, I cannot help but be observant about local church (Protestant, Catholic) or even native "syncretistic" traditions (like Shakers, Santo Daime, Santería, the Maria Lionsa devotees, etc.), taking time to consider their origin and effectiveness for the People. As a priest, but also as a continuing inquirer into all things spiritual, I have always found it rewarding to be aware of how a local church or religious group experiences itself. Wherever they live out their particular culture or tradition, Native People have much to share with us.

What is a journey? Or, for that matter, what is a *sacred* journey? Perhaps there are many different answers to these questions; each one might describe a particular passage that someone has taken or one that must be undertaken by any of us. My own life journey is that of a Catholic priest with its plethora of daily sacred and mundane activities, and this singular tour of life has allowed me to travel among women, men, and children of just about every human culture. In their individuality and uniqueness of spirit many have shared their dreams with me and, moreover, helped me to dream. To dream, I would venture to say, is to be subliminally active with the future possibilities of life itself.

As we human beings move about from day to day, we do so in relation to everything else that exists for us. At times, we might think we are the only ones concerned, but in actual fact we are not alone in our universe, neither in our own personal universe nor the one that contains vast galaxies of interstellar space. It seems that whatever exists actually expresses itself in some kind of movement, either self-motivated or caused by other beings, other existences, nearby. Motion even occurs at the molecular level. Both scientists and spiritual people from ancient times to this day assure us of the reality of movement. Human movement itself indicates, points to, all forms of life. Some movement means expressing one's inner self, as in a dance; another signifies wandering about with no specific purpose in mind; while another kind of movement might mean journeying forth so as to enter into a deeper reality of existence:

> *Both are important,*
> *The Journey and the Dream,*
> *The coming out and the entering in.*
>
> *Without the Journey*
> *The Dream is a futile entering into yourself*

Where you ride a monotonous wheel
That spins around you alone.

With the Journey
The entering in is itself a Journey
That does not end inside you
But passes through the self and
Out the other side of you
Where you ride the wheel
You found inside.

To remain inside too long
Makes the Journey a fairytale Odyssey
And the Dream becomes illusion.
The wheel must spin on the real road
Where your Dream leads you.

To remain on the road too long
Dims the Dream until you no longer see it
And the road replaces the Dream.

The Journey and the Dream
Are one balanced act of love
And both are realized
Outside the mind.

—Murray Bodo, O.F.M.,
Francis: The Journey and the Dream

So, come, travel with me for a while and I will tell you where I have been, who has been with me, and what we have done. The One who makes all *dreams* and all *journeys* possible urges us to get on board!

England

Early Life

My *journey* began when I was born in the well-known Highgate Hospital, London, England on August 23, 1947, in the second year of recovery efforts after World War II had ended. Two *dream*ers in love brought me into being. My father, John McCarthy, was born in the celebrated town of Doneraile, County Cork, Ireland. A man always close to the earth, he experienced the daily joy of tending to flowers and other plants in his beautiful gardens wherever he lived throughout his life. My mother, Margaret McMahon, was born in Glasgow, Scotland. Her own special joy showed itself in her openness to friendships with many people and her closeness to her own family. Both were bearers of positive hope wherever they went. They *dream*ed again and my brother Anthony came to us two years later to start his *journey* and I am grateful that we are still in close proximity to each other so as to be able to get together often.

My dad, John, Jersey Island, England, 1940

As Catholics we were always very interested in our faith and I have several memories of going to Mass in cathedrals, various other churches around London, as well as being involved in our local parish of Our Lady and Saint Joseph and its parochial school.

John McCarthy, Bombay, India, 1939

I gradually became aware of other local churches and denominations and people of other world faiths. I was taught respect for others at an early age, and this has always helped me even to this day.

I had a wonderful life as a child. Mum and Dad lavished attention on us. Our home was always open to visitors and dinners and parties were usual for us. I remember Mom or Dad often inviting to our house various individuals who had a homeland in one of the former distant British colonies like British Columbia or Australia or one of the African countries. I always knew that I lived in what nowadays one might call a multilingual, multicultural world and that was just fine with me. In 1953 Elizabeth II became queen of the United Kingdom and all seemed well from my point of view as a child.

Art and architecture, as well as music, have always had a hold on me. In London there is just so much to see and do, whether one is a child or an adult. Perhaps most children are interested in cartoons and drawings, especially if they are drawn on behalf of children and especially if they are educative, that is, if they help the children to become just a little bit more interested in some of the unique aspects of life. I was one of these children who always looked forward to the weekend newspaper with its special section of "funnies" dedicated to children. Two particular comic strips were

Wedding day, Isle of Wight, England, 1946

especially interesting for me at the time, one about a Scottish boy called Rory from one of the ancient highland clans (he was perhaps my age, I thought) who had an eagle as a friend, and another that chronicled the seventeenth and eighteenth century interactions between Huron and Iroquois First Nations and the relations between these tribes and the French and English (I am not exactly sure who I identified with most back then since politics had no hold on me) who were dueling over what is now Canada and part of the United States of America.

Piccadilly Square, London, 1956

From my place in England's capital, I often used my imagination to enter the worlds of these interesting kinds of individuals, human beings who were different because of the historical time period as well as because of their culture and ambiance. I was intrigued by a world beyond my own comfortable home not so far from the center of London. In earlier times this capital city certainly had exercised both positive and negative controls on a colony far and away across the sea as well as on Scotland, another supposed colony of English influence to the north.

American movies, often portraying Native People from prejudicial and cultural lack of understanding perspectives, were shown to children every Saturday morning at the local neighborhood cinema. Of course, I also enjoyed going with my brother Tony and our friends, as did everyone else. Yet even as a young child, I sensed that much of the content in movies coming from the U.S.A. was "make believe." But it was lots of fun for a child of my age.

Even though at that period of my life I had not yet met any native People from Canada or the United States, I remember distinctly being interested and looked forward to visiting these lands so distant from me. During this early part of my life I learned that it is good to be open-minded, alert, and ready to go forward each day, trusting that there is "something ahead" that each one of us can enter into that will teach us how to live life authentically. Perhaps I was beginning my *journey* with little steps. Nonetheless, I had a feeling that my *dreams* were somehow influencing me. Or did I just like to sleep in on the weekends! I am not really sure now.

London, England, 1953

Canada

The New Land

In 1957 we immigrated to Canada, more specifically to Toronto, Ontario. It is here that the eagle of the comic strip and the Native People portrayed in the movies were transformed into realities for me. Along with everyone else in this new land of mine, now I came to live in a place where eagles flew freely and those who especially appreciated them, women, men, and children of the First Nations, were also not so distant from me. The unique history and culture of Canada, somewhat different from the British version that I had already experienced in my young life, became real in ways that I could more easily understand. Perhaps I was just growing up and learning wonderfully new things in interesting new ways.

Immigration is a family effort, one that is not usually easy for all of the individuals concerned. Many little decisions help make up a larger decision to immigrate. As I look back on it now, for my Dad there were two factors helping him decide to move us from the mother country to another in the Commonwealth.

The first had to do with economics. Post World War II England was not an easy place to be for many young families. Rationing of food items like meat and orange juice, not much money to spend on extra items and little pleasures, and a great need for immediate housing due to bomb destruction was reality for many folks in countless larger cities as well as smaller towns of the realm.

The international effects of the war economy and its aftermath occasioned those seeking stable employment and good living conditions to flood to England from the remaining British colonies and the

Commonwealth. It was a great mix of people; on the other hand, it was also a clash-of-cultures experience for many.

Due to war the national psyche had become damaged; yet it was not broken. A new spirit of relief and reconstruction was very much alive in Britain. Even so, a good number of families decided to leave Britain in order to seek a better life within some of the countries of the Commonwealth. Our family had several choices of places to go, it seemed. We even went to see government-sponsored films of some of these countries. My Dad seemed to fix his desire on Canada rather than South Africa or Australia or New Zealand. Some of his Irish acquaintances thought the same and so they made plans to fly ahead together to a new land of opportunity in order to prepare a place for their families. While still in England the three of us looked forward to his weekly airmail letters telling us about his experiences in that faraway place that was to become our home.

The second factor had to do with a sheer sense of adventure, a desire to explore new places in order to know new people and make new friends. I suppose that my Dad was always a kind of vagabond or potential world traveler, always looking for something interesting around the corner for himself and for his family. Mom was less interested in traveling, but trusted Dad in all of this; I believe that she always helped temper his decisions with her own input. Prior to the war, as a single man he had worked as a waiter on board the famous luxury liner of that time, The Queen Mary, which is now docked as a tourist attraction in Long Beach, California. Later on, while we were still living in London, he worked a short cruise trip around the Mediterranean. Through well-animated travel stories that interested us profoundly, he encouraged us to think about the whole world as our home, to be comfortable in it, no matter where we happened to be. I think that I have taken after him in my desire to travel. I do indeed feel at home in many places.

Crossing the Atlantic Sea

Our crossing of the Atlantic Sea in 1957 to our new Canadian home was unforgettable for a number of reasons. After leaving the English port of Southampton, an unexpected stop at the French coastal town of Le Havre was made. Our ship, the *Ascania,* evidently had been asked to take on board what seemed to me to be about 1000 Hungarian refugees fleeing communism that had recently taken over their country. We were not told of this beforehand. Some of the paying passengers complained bitterly about this situation and wanted to continue on, leaving them behind for other ships to come to their aid. While the refugees were being processed on board, we spent the day exploring the town where, quite surprisingly, my mother ran into a fellow Scotswoman who graciously invited us to tea in her nearby home. As none of our family spoke French, this was a good thing for us to do.

These same refugees suffered greatly on board our ship, I believe. Two days after they had joined us, as I chanced to explore the upper decks, I saw many of them in complete misery. They had only a few blankets among them and a good number were vomiting from their deck chairs. We later discovered they had been given no cabins of any kind and so were at the mercy of the Atlantic Sea's great squalls, not to mention the disturbing motion of the ship on the waves. Vomit, urine, and feces were spread all over the deck. Men women and children were quite ill, it seemed to me. If truth be told, it was a pitiful sight, even for a child like me. Possibly it was my first real experience of apparent human injustice.

This experience also formed within me a great compassion for the plight of refugees, wherever they exist in our world. After having suffered another day or two of this kind of treatment that is not even due to animals, a number of the Hungarians rioted, breaking into some of the empty cabins and hallways, loudly demanding just treatment from the ship's officers. I am not really sure what they really got, but things seemed to have calmed down shortly thereafter. Even as that moment of fear took its temporary hold on me, I also sensed that these people deserved much better treatment.

In our own time we hear much about refugees, people fleeing zones of war and violence or starvation in their own "third world" countries. Our planet may be large in size, yet it is nevertheless also small in other ways, and opportunities to respond in kindness by individuals, organizations, or governments are myriad. "There but for the grace of God go you or I" always holds true, I firmly believe. Our human interconnectedness calls out to us to respond to the needs of those who suffer. Sometimes just one little bit of sincere compassion at a time will indeed go a long way to help.

I might add that several years later, while on the job helping my dad paint an apartment in Long Beach, California, I ran into an elderly Hungarian man who, as proved by the details of our conversation, was present on the very same ship, the *Ascania,* that my family had travelled on decades before. As we spoke together of some of the incidences of long ago, I noticed tears forming in his eyes. At that self-same moment our histories had merged once again, even though our individual journeys were many years apart. Such coincidences in life, happenstances, are amazing to me when they occur, and I have experienced not a few of them. *The journey and the dream* are constantly connected.

A Very Different Terrain

Our new home was to be in Downsview, a solid brick house on the outskirts of Toronto. In front of us and behind there were uncountable fields of trees and bushes with enough "wild" animals and birds to satisfy the interests of an erstwhile city boy: skunks, rabbits, raccoons, opossums, coyotes, snakes, hawks, ravens, red-winged blackbirds and ... even eagles!

We soon discovered a nearby swampy lake at which we spent many hours swimming or rafting, noticing up-close dragonflies and beautiful little birds. The setting was ideal and we could easily step into the past and imagine it as also a site for homes belonging to Native Peoples from the distant past, especially those of the Iroquois Confederation, the *Haudenosaunee*. In the winter we skated on nearby frozen ponds, even at night. We loved

Testing "Indian" bows and arrows with Dad and brother Tony on left. Toronto, Ontario, Canada, 1958

to toboggan and sled and to follow snow trails of little animals and birds, coming to recognize them by the unique footprints that they left behind. It was a magical world for me as I approached my teen years.

Every Saturday or Sunday Dad would drive us somewhere special, often it to a somewhat distant lake or town. It was always fun making new friends and doing the usual things of kids our age. I have fond memories visiting a large family of fellow émigrés who had settled in Brantford, Ontario. From my studies in school I was already aware that the town was named after Joseph Brant (Thayendanegea, 1743–1807), an Iroquois leader who had helped the British in colonial times. The Iroquois reservation ("reserve" in Canada) Oshweken was situated nearby. I looked forward to visiting it some day.

First Contacts

That day came. I mentioned what I knew about the place to our friends in Brantford and asked if they knew any Indian families nearby. Sure enough, they did. So they took me to a house down the street belonging to a Mohawk family. Though I do not remember their names, I vividly can call to mind their hospitality. Evidently, like

Ready for Sunday church, Toronto, Ontario, Canada, 1959

With brother Tony exploring the "wilderness" of Ontario, Canada, 1959

many occasions in my life, I had shown up just in time for dinner and so without hesitation they invited me to eat with them. A lot of people were sitting around the table. The dad prayed and then we feasted. In front of me were platters of bread, fish, meat, salad, and bowls of corn, beans, and squash. These last three are known by Native Peoples of the east as "the three sisters" and their seeds are traditionally planted together in the same mound of earth. As time goes by, corn grows straight up, allowing the bean vines to attach themselves to its stalk, while the leaves of the squash spread out, protecting the soil from becoming overly parched by the sun. These three plants are symbolic of mutual cooperation.

How our contemporary world needs to learn from the helpful togetherness of these three plant sisters! Though each plant, like a country or an individual, has the ability to live and grow alone, it is much better for all concerned if things are done together for mutual benefit. We have much to learn from plants.

The table conversation answered lots of my questions about Native life, and to my surprise, the father of the family invited me to go with him to see Oshweken for a short visit. My heart was overjoyed by the invitation. And so, right after dinner we left. It was a short tour of some traditional longhouses, a Mohawk Anglican chapel, the river, and a house that was the home of a well-known movie star of the time, Jay Silverheels who played Tonto in the popular series, *The Lone Ranger.* He was in actuality a Mohawk born on the Six Nations Reserve, being given the name Harold J. Smith (1912–1980). I was charged up by the experience and longed for more adventures.

The saying holds true that in life "one thing leads to another." Spiritually speaking, and upon looking deeper into "what's really going on," one might also say that all things are connected and that such relationship can take on special meaning for us. We human beings always seek out meaning from moment to moment as we relate to what is happening all around us in our circles of life. Any one of us may choose to give special significance to events and situations that come up each day. Nevertheless, for a lot of us there is an underlying feeling, or a not so easily explainable innate knowledge, that life is guided by some "higher power." I have come to believe that the highest power that we might name as Creator, *Akbaatadia, Wakan Tanka, Allah,* or God, does so in, with, and through our own free will choices. So as we opt to "see" connections between one thing and another, or recognize relationships among the myriads of beings, quite often we are led to trust in a connection with that Highest Power who makes everything possible. This helps us make sense of *the journey and the dream.*

INDIANCRAFTS

I have a talent for working with my hands. I like to design things and enjoy making things, items large or small. I like to dream about possibilities. I enjoy art in any form, but especially architecture. I appreciate what I see with my eyes, what I touch, what I can hear and feel and taste; and I love to read—all kinds of books. On *the journey* books help to feed *the dreams*.

I began to visit local libraries and bookmobiles, always looking for a good selection of literature dealing with Native subjects. A few books showed how one might learn to make or copy some everyday items of the Native world like clothing, drums, rattles, etc. Some showed how to tan animal skins in the traditional way or how to prepare and decorate feathers for headdresses and personal adornment. Many books were well known in the scouting movement, especially to those inducted into the Order of the Arrow. Non-Native people in these movements took their crafting of Indian items quite seriously and did their best to make items according to the ancient ways or learn to dance and sing at powwows and other gatherings. Of course, from the beginning it was the Native People who taught them how. But in the scheme of things, as time went by authors like W. Ben Hunt *(The Golden Book of Indiancrafts)* and Bernard Stirling Mason *(Indian Crafts and Costumes)* had become well known in this area of activity

My display at Downsview Library, Toronto, Canada, 1961

With my brother Tony, wearing my first examples of handiwork, Toronto, Canada, 1961

First powwow regalia that I made, Toronto, Canada, 1961

long before I came to try my hand at creating Native heritage items for myself and friends.

One day, while at the local library, I was approached by a librarian who asked why I was taking out so many books about Indians. I told him I was learning about some of these crafts by myself through books because there was no Native person nearby to teach me. He asked me to bring in some items made by me for him to see. And so I brought forth a warbonnet made with imitation eagle feathers and some rattles and carvings that I had spent many hours making. He seemed so pleased that a young kid had such an intense interest in Indian culture that he created a special display of my works to encourage other young people to do similar things.

Iroquois Pageant

A local newspaper reporter happened to go into the library, saw the display, and asked to meet me in order to do a story on me. As a result of the interview for that article he offered to take me to see the outdoor Six Nations Pageant. It just happened to be playing that Friday night at the reserve near Brantford. He also suggested that we bring along some of the things that I had made. I suppose now that he was really looking for another follow-up newspaper story.

Across from our house, Dad and brother Tony wearing the first headdress I made. Toronto, Ontario, Canada, 1960

DOWNSVIEW

Scot-Indian At Library

The Downsview branch of the North York Public Library is featuring a display of Indian craft created by a 14-year-old boy.

Cornelius McCarthy of Downsview has such items as a Sioux war club, leggings, arrows, a chief's headdress and a colorful ceremonial shield.

He became interested in Indian lore several years ago while at public school in Downsview.

Now a grade nine student at St. Michael's College, Cornelius is especially fascinated with the Sioux tribe.

Occasionally when things are quiet at the library, a Scottish clerk tries on some of the Indian clothes.

Last week, several people choosing books were served by a tall Scotsman with a very broad accent, dressed as a Sioux Indian.

Needless to say, they got the wrong book.

Telegram

If you see a man with an Indian chief's headdress stamp your card at the North York Public Library—don't head for the hills. It's just librarian Doug Bowers getting into the spirit of the special display of Indian craft at the library. Here Doug shows Mrs. Joan Gehl a choice item in the display created by 14-year-old Cornelius McCarthy of Downsview. Especially fascinated by the Sioux tribe, Cornelius has such items as war clubs, leggings, arrows and a chief's headdress.

Local newspaper article, Toronto, Ontario, Canada, 1962

With a whoop, Scotty McCarthy models one of his Indian costumes.

Local newspaper article, Toronto, Ontario, Canada, 1962

Teen-Ager Studies Indian Life

By **HERBERT BRYCE**

A Toronto student has made an Indian war bonnet which is so realistic that a full-blooded Indian near Chicago offered him $35 for it.

Cornelius (Scotty) McCarthy recently displayed his bonnet, with 10 other items of a chief's costume, at a Knights of Columbus arts and crafts contest. The judges awarded him a white ribbon as a special tribute to his handmade costume.

It includes headdresses, leggings, chief's cape, moccasins, coupe stick (trophy stick) and a war club of the Sioux tribe. The costume is now displayed at the North York Library after a two-month showing at the Downsview branch of the Toronto Public Libraries.

"I want to explain that the Indians were peaceful people," Scotty says. "I want to tell what they were really like. There were good Indians and bad Indians—I want people to know about the good ones."

Scotty started his hobby about two years ago when he became angry because Indians on television programs were invariably portrayed as cruel savages.

He began a study of North American Indians, and spent hours delving through old books, encyclopedias and magazines. He has collected half a dozen scrap books full of newspaper clippings about Indians, is constantly ordering booklets from the Queen's Printer and fairly haunts the U.S. Department of the Interior with his letters requesting information.

So far he has concentrated on the crafts of the Sioux. "They were the most colorful of the Plains Indians," he contends.

Right now he is working on a horned war bonnet. "It has a big trail of feathers," he says. He finds that he must substitute many materials. For instance, the Roach's headdress now on display at the library he describes as a row of porcupine bristles on the head, worn by the Woodland tribes so their war bonnets would not become entangled in the trees. Scotty used a fibre material because he could not catch enough porcupines. Many of his materials, such as leather, he gets from arts and crafts shops.

The 15-year-old St. Michael's College student wore his regalia at the Six Nations pageant at Brantford this summer, and took part in the dances with the celebrating Indians.

"They were glad I came," he says. "They were glad that a white person was interested."

Scotty says that the chiefs encouraged him when he said he wanted to help them. He hopes to write about them, and would like to have a newspaper column on how to make Indian crafts.

"I want to write about them as an Indian sees them, not as the white man sees them."

He plans eventually to enter the Citizenship Department's Indian Affairs branch. In the meantime, he has joined the Toronto Indian Club which is open to anyone interested in Indian culture.

He has visited the Indians at Brantford and near Chicago, and corresponds with one he met in Wisconsin. He is compiling information to write a book about the cultural areas of North American India[illegible]

It was a long drive. But upon arrival, we were welcomed by some of the Native folks in charge of putting on the pageant. Seeing what I had brought with me, they told me to quickly put on the regalia and become part of the drama. What joy and exhilaration I felt as I was invited to step into a real birch bark canoe (something that I had only read about or seen pictures of in books) and glide across the water in one of the scenes. Afterwards some photos were taken that I treasure to this day.

As I recall, the pageant was a kind of reenactment of Iroquois history, especially about the coming of Deganawideh (the Peacemaker) who helped to bring the five tribes (Mohawk, Onondaga, Seneca, Oneida, Cayuga) into the *Haudensaunee*. Later, the Tuscaroras joined them to complete the Six Nations. At that time who, Native or other, would have thought that this kind of "intercultural sharing" would push me further to seek more of *the journey and the dream* of my life? In retrospect, perhaps the event was, according to our more modern standards, a bit "touristically theatric," but, at least for me, it helped to further my acquaintances with Native People, especially some Mohawks.

Because of that reporter's second article, a local TV station invited me to be interviewed on one of their host-led shows. Wow! I had never expected anything like this to happen to me. Besides, I would be getting a day off school! It is interesting to consider how in life one person can really influence another. The little kindnesses that we do for one another really can help someone else fulfill much of their life plan. I owe a lot to that anonymous reporter of long ago.

I also remember that one time when I was an eighth grader my brother and I participated in a kind of talent show at school. We must have been pretty daring at the time, our regalia not really being up to par. He drummed and I performed my version of an eagle dance. We probably needed a lot more practice because my own movements did not jive so well with his intermittent drum beats. Needless to say, it got mixed reviews and a lot of laughs, even though we were quite serious about our performance at the time.

On one of our early vacations as a family we visited the well-known Algonquin Park, a vast area of protected woods and lakes and rivers and hills set aside as part of the Canadian patrimony for

With Six Nations Pageant participants, Brantford, Ontario, 1961

all to enjoy. To me it seemed like a preternatural place, fully alive, replete with ancient history. Along the way we stopped by some kind of trading post that had a large area set apart with a wonderful, authentic looking set of Huron or Iroquois longhouses. Inside, the houses were subdivided for different family dwelling places and were complete with tanned hides, cornhusks, cooking utensils and sleeping areas. Only the living Native families seemed to be missing.

"A house is not a home," we often hear. We need people to make the important sounds of tears and laughter echo off structured walls. They need to move about and touch those same walls and hang pictures and photographic memories on them. They must cook and share food at a common table. They need also to have time to reflect and dream on comfortable beds at day's end. They must also be able to rise up the following morning to greet the new day with all of its responsibilities. A home allows for all these activities. Here cherished memories are continually made. A house-become-home is always much more than a renovated building or a finely detailed reconstruction of a past reality. A home is a place of growth, a womb of development, a great cauldron brimming with possibilities. It is a place where each day *the journey* is planned according to the instructions of *the dream*.

Canadian History

In school I learned about early French and English explorers and the fur trade that took place between them and the tribes. The *courier de bois*, the "runners of the woods" who were Europeans, mixed bloods, and First Nations People formed quite a network over the years, allowing animal pelts to be traded across long distances over and over again until they reached France and other European destinations. These journeys were difficult and dangerous, requiring much walking, making a *portage* (carrying canoes from one river or lake to another), and canoeing with heavy loads in often inclement weather, sometimes hostile people nearby. Once delivered to their destination points, the hides were then turned into clothing and felt products. In exchange, local Natives received trade cloth, beads, metal axes, pots and pans, and decorative items worked in silver, copper, and brass.

Not so far from where we lived was a shrine to the "Canadian Martyrs," named after the slain French Jesuits who shared their faith and culture with Huron and Iroquois People as well as other tribes. The heroic activities of these brave and deeply spiritual men were remembered in all the history books. I was intrigued to visit a few of these places, as was my family.

Some of them were Isaac Jogues (1607-1646), Jean de Brebeuf (1594–1649), and Gabriel Lalemant (1610–1649), who were assisted by many companions, both Native and non-Native, giving their utmost for what they believed in. A contemporary film, *Blackrobe,* describes the culture-shock situations that both they and their Native friends experienced in that time. Even today they are honored as saints by Catholics and others, both Native and non-Native.

About that time I also learned about *Kateri Tekakwitha* ("Katherine," "The One Who Puts Everything in Order," 1656–1680), a young Mohawk woman who listened to the missionaries, blending her new faith with the ancient ways of her people as many others have done throughout the centuries. In this regard, I might mention that I have come to know another Native woman of faith, Sister Kateri Mitchell, who for a number of years has headed up the Tekakwitha Conference. This spiritual association strives to unify Native Catholic voice, presence, and identity while respecting the diversity of the People.

It also tries to deepen these things and affirm cultural and spiritual traditions. At the same time, this respected gathering of the People communicates among them and involves them in the life of the Catholic Church. It is also ecumenical in scope, as it should be.

Some events in life are like the links of a chain. More recently on my travels it was quite a surprise for me to meet a young girl who also proudly carries the name Kateri. I met her just about four years ago in southern Guyana. She and her mother help the Jesuit pastor at Saint Ignatius Mission located close by the town of Lethem, just below the Rupununi Mountains. She is a member of the Wapeshana Tribe. A naming tradition continues on in ways that one would not usually expect, as there is such a great distance in time and space and culture from the first Kateri to the young woman living in the jungles of Guyana, South America. Kateri's spirit must truly live on in her People wherever they are found.

Grammar school history books, as well as a Canadian television series of the time, told of two early French explorers of the New World (New France). Pierre-Esprit Radisson (1636-1710) and his brother-in-law Médard Chouart Sieur des Groseilliers (1618-1696) moved together among the various woodland tribes, finally reaching the Chippewas (Anishnabe) as they followed what is now called the Flambeau Trail throughout much of present-day state of Wisconsin. In my dreams and wishes I certainly would have liked to be given a chance to voyage along with them.

I can easily remember getting up very early on many a Saturday morning in order to take the bus into Toronto to visit the Royal Ontario Provincial Museum. It was a joy for me to visit this well-known city landmark because it showed art and artifacts from the world of Canadian (and for that matter, North American) Indian cultures. From paintings by Paul Kane to totem poles and a headdress that once belonged to Sitting Bull, there was much to see, admire, and take within oneself. Trips to this museum and the surrounding downtown area were like a weekly college education opportunity for me. Here there was no rush to study and no exams to take.

I even recall making an appointment to visit the main curator of the Indian cultures section who was a well-known anthropologist and ethnologist. I thought that my future life work would be in some kind of anthropology relating to Native Peoples. Once I got in to see him I was so nervous that I forgot exactly what I had wanted to say because he had been watching me, evidently quite amused that someone so young should actually come to his special study. He patiently waited for a while and then kindly ushered me into a private museum library reserved only for the experts. I had never expected this special privilege. Now at last I had access to books and journals that went much deeper into things "Indian" than the ones perused at the local library. After that day, I knew that in some way I was destined to be involved in Native affairs. But, how exactly, I was not so sure. In retrospect I now know that there was indeed a *journey* happening here but first I needed to become more conscious of *the dream*.

My grammar school was named after Saint Charles Borromeo, a great ecclesiastical reformer and saint. The nuns teaching there were from Loretto Abbey. Often our classes were really livened up when we were visited by priests who shared with us wonderful stories of what they were doing in their work and ministry in far away places or even nearby in our archdiocese. Sometimes these priests were missionaries, often those involved throughout Canada and its Northwest Territories, like the OMIs (Order of Mary Immaculate) or even the C.S.Sp.s (Congregation of the Holy Spirit or Holy Ghost Fathers) who really impressed us with their white Algerian-style habits that included a fascinating kind of hat called a *fez* in Arabic. The school principal, Mother St. Philip, was sure that I should join one of these religious orders to become a priest who worked with Native People. This was her desire, but it is not exactly the route that I later took. I was too involved in being a young eighth grader and having a fun social life with friends of my same age group. As I look back now I realize that *the journey* for me was just beginning because good *and* interesting individuals were helping me to create *the dream*.

Sometime after John Fitzgerald Kennedy came into office as president of the United States of America, my parents gave me a large book just published called *The American Heritage Book of Indians* by William Brandon. This was a welcome gift for it allowed me a deeper knowledge of North American Indian history. Sometime later I donated it, along with some other similar books, to a newly-built Indian Friendship Center in Toronto. It was a large and fine looking

Second home,
Toronto, Ontario, Canada, 1962

building. The gifts were appreciated and I felt a good connection with my new friends. Nowadays I know that there are many such Native-to-Native places across Canada, even in the United States and some other countries, that welcome those on their journey to somewhere else or those who are locals and just want to make some good ties with fellow Natives who understand their spiritual ways and needs. These special folks who run these kinds of centers should be held in high regard because they not only dream of possibilities, but also help others to *dream* about what is next on their own particular *journey*. We have a lot to learn from these centers of resting and healing. Our larger world, especially in its multicultural context, could also benefit from well-staffed, wisely-planned zones of recuperation, sites of personal and communal creativity, places that allow for human connectivity. Adults and children together need such places in our lives.

Children, I believe, are naturally spiritual and should always be allowed to pursue the ways of the Spirit. Depending on how they are reared, children have that innate sense of desiring to participate in the "more" of life, to express some sense of a developing "destiny', a wanting to live life fully, in spite of any personal and environmental limitations. Adults, being older chronologically, always have opportunities to influence children in such ways as to help them seek out what is best for them. Grandparents, teachers, and friends of children know the importance of non-controlling, positive influence with children of all ages. The Native way is to try to consider, when planning anything important, the effects of present day plans on the next seven generations of human beings. This is especially difficult to live out nowadays because most of us, and especially children, live in a fast-food, fast lane, fast-response, fast-result, kind of culture which seems to primarily value the present moment, not caring to peer too deeply into the future.

California

Another New Home

As I indicated earlier, my dad must have been born with a spirit of travel and adventure inside his being. I believe that I have inherited a measure of that spirit, just as Prophet Elias in good time came to receive a good measure of Elijah's spirit of prophecy.

The summer of 1964 found us, a car full of Torontonians, traveling south and west all the way to Los Angeles, California on the myriad roads of the famous Route 66. We were on vacation—or so it seemed to my brother Tony and me. Little did we know that ahead of time Mom and Dad had already prepared immigration papers for us all so that we could immediately take up permanent residence

Newly arrived immigrants on Signal Hill, near Long Beach, California, 1964

in our new country called the United States of America. We found all this out upon arriving at our destination. Had we known this before we left Canada, Tony and I would have really put up a fight to keep from leaving. Dad had been lured by the prospect of better employment and the reality of leaving behind all the cold, snowy winters with their incessant traffic jams and accidents. *The journey*, it seemed, was now taking a different route than the one in my *dream*, I felt.

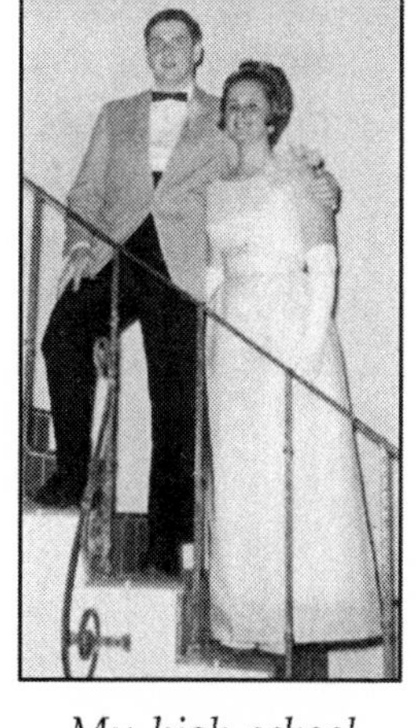

My high school Prom Night, 1965

But then the sunny beaches and alluring postcard perfect palm trees seemed to call out to us to make our new home near them. We settled in Long Beach, where Saint Anthony High, a school with a fine reputation for scholarship as well as for fun, became my alma mater. Informally it was also known as a place that produced a lot of vocations to the Catholic priesthood. At the time I did not know this, but after graduation in 1966 I indeed became one of those seminary statistics. In the fall I entered Saint John's Seminary College, Camarillo.

Graduation, St. Anthony High School, Long Beach, California, 1966

Though in certain ways I was pleased with this part of my *dream, the journey*ing was difficult. Though a time of growth for me, it was at the same time a bittersweet period. Just a few short years after decisions were made by the world's bishops and pope at the Second Vatican Council to proceed with "aggiornamento" (to renew, to update the world-wide Catholic Church), not all church "institutions," like seminaries preparing men for the priesthood, were ready to make

Seminary student Scott, St. John's College, Camarillo, California, 1966

the required huge paradigmatic changes. I know that most of us were caught in the situation of a Church that was undergoing mighty change both from within and from without. We are still going through these changes, and even now not all of them are welcomed by everyone. As for me, I have come to realize that "there is room under the roof for everyone," no matter how they relate to the ecclesiastical changes that affect their lives.

A year and a half later the faculty and I mutually recognized that it was not the place for me; and so I left, moving on to attend Long Beach City College. For me, this was a time of great soul-searching and life-goal decision making. I came to understand more deeply the value of prayer. Perhaps it was a bit like Saint John of the Cross's "dark night of the soul." After a semester I was accepted at another seminary, Saint Patrick's College, Mountain View, not too far from San Francisco.

Certain people become special mentors in our lives at those special times that they are most needed. Their influence lives on in us throughout our lives and we are the better for it. Some are definitely good listeners, others excel in offering a word of wisdom at the right moment, while some are just around us and do not even know that they are influencing us for the better. We observe the activities of their lives. I have been blessed by many such people. Among them are Father Al Giaquinto S.S., an innovative pioneer of contemporary seminary formation, Annemarie and Ed Schmitz, and Michael Hoerni (r.i.p.). From my formative college years until now I have carried them in my heart. Their great generosity over the many years has carried me forward: a delicious meal once in a while, special trips to both educate and be enjoyed, ears that really listen to me, prayers that lift me up. I know that they have mentored many others as well. May they be blessed forever!

To support myself I helped my dad with his painting and decorating business. I met a lot of nice people on our jobs. We painted the homes of the rich and the dwellings of the poor; we gave all the houses a better look, both inside and outside, whether in the ghetto areas or in the richer neighborhoods. It did not matter. My dad was honest, and I wanted to follow his example. I learned a lot about people in those days of paintbrush and roller and I made

My birthday feast at an Irish castle, 1970

lots of friends, as did my dad. I came to appreciate up close interior design, color, texture, and all kinds of architecture. We never had to advertise. Dad became well known to many people in Long Beach and its environs. I learned to be generous like him. I gained important knowledge about generosity and its ensuing blessings. Many are the times that he painted an elderly widow's room or house for much, much less than he needed to charge; and he always kept it a secret from them lest they became embarrassed. Mom, who I always knew was also quite proud of me, nursed at Saint Mary's Hospital. She would often, to my feigned embarrassment, introduce me to her special patients when I went to pick her up at night after her shift. These experiences in the hospital have helped me greatly as I continue to relate to the folks in the ministry of the sick, whether in hospital or home.

For each person growing up, maturing into the next stage of life, the growth process is not always easy. But it is necessary and can be enjoyable. I know that, like other human beings, there were difficult moments that I would rather not call to mind. Now such memories do not seem to really bother me. I acknowledge them, try to understand them in their own particular context, and then usually move forward from them in order to concentrate on more positive aspects of life. Perhaps in this matter I have gleaned from both my parents who, I know, suffered a lot of external tragedy during the war years and yet always stayed positive in the face of difficulty. They experienced many metamorphoses in their own lives and, looking back, so have I. Like them, I have always tried to share my *joie de vivre* with others in the good times and in the bad.

I really enjoyed my high school years—the friends, the studies, the teachers, the football games, and especially the dances afterwards. I made many friends and there always was a lot to do. Ours was a home where hospitality was supreme. Every day somebody came to see us. Sometimes I was a bit put off if some of my peers rang the doorbell looking to visit with my folks instead of just me. But it was not that bad. I came to realize that my friends just liked being around my parents who were so outgoing and not so judgmental of others. Besides, there was always free food and drink available for them.

While still in between seminaries, I recall one time being invited to a large Order of the Arrow gathering at one of the stadiums in Long Beach. There were some wonderful displays of Indian drumming and dancing and colorful regalia. It was the closest thing to a powwow that I had experienced. The special guest was an old movie star that I had read about and seen in many movies: Iron Eyes

At Stonehenge, England, 1971

Visiting an Irish castle with Dad, 1971

Cody (1904–1999). I shook hands with him, taking note of his fine regalia. Years later I was to hear that he was not really what he portrayed himself to be as a Native American. Whoever he actually was, and however he portrayed himself (even as a "Hollywood Indian"), I understand that, even apart from his movies, he always promoted Indian ways. He married an Indian woman, and raised two sons. The taller one, Tree Cody, is quite accomplished as a cedar flute player. I have seen him several times at different powwows in Montana.

My autographed photo of Iron Eyes Cody

CALIFORNIA TRIBES

As time passed, I learned about some of the California tribes and their bittersweet existence under Spanish temporal and religious rule. With this subject I am somewhat conflicted. A part of me wants to say that the survival of their cultural heritage to this day is due to their heroic tenacity; and many of their spiritual ways certainly are still practiced as a result of their own efforts; but I also feel that friendships made with a good number of Franciscan missionaries were beneficial in these areas as well, though not necessarily with all those past religious leaders. The other part of me is not so sure of what to think about the past: what is said to be true and what is said to be not true in the oral tradition and in books. Those times were much different from our own. I believe that in any era human beings from any culture are quite capable of looking for and receiving in return the good that is within others. This can happen even as both are experiencing "culture shock."

Most of the twenty-one California missions are thriving modern Catholic parishes and, besides tourists, they provide for the spiritual welfare of many people each day, although perhaps the Native clientele, whose ancestors actually built the mission structures and maintained them along with the Franciscan padres, is less visible than before. Happily, efforts continue to be made among members of the tribes, like those of the Rumsen (Ohlone), Amah Mutsun (Ohlone), Salinan, Esselen, and Chumash and others as well, to reclaim part of their spiritual heritage at the missions. One example of this is my own diocese, Monterey. Our bishop, Richard Garcia, is most interested in furthering the causes of Native People. A good number of local requests are being attended to in regard to maintenance of burial sites, indigenous ceremonies, and acculturation in the liturgy.

I believe that many tribes in this state have been devastated several times over. First by the Spanish invaders, then by the thousands of people who flooded into their lands at the time of the Gold Rush and its aftermath, and again in our own time when folks from all over the world, including people from other states, have come looking for a better life, both economically and otherwise. Many of these newcomers do not even know that tribes still exist in California in these modern times. They certainly are neither interested in the tribal histories, nor in the People's present activities, other than to try their luck in some of the tribal casinos. Knowing that California is a land of earthquakes, one might say that tremors from past human-caused earthquakes still bother the People of this state. When will the next aftershock happen?, one might ask.

While in my seminary training, from about 1966-1973, I encountered several fellow young men preparing to become priests who were also proud of their own Native heritage. Some actually went on to be ordained and now serve in different parts of the country. It seems that wherever I went there was some kind of contact with Native People who had varying degrees of connection to their own tribal histories.

Dear reader, in the following pages may I now begin to relate something of who I have become through more than thirty-five years of ministerial service? I would need many reams of paper to record all of God's goodness to me down through the years. As I mark out some significant lines of my life with you, permit me also to introduce some Native People, who along with everyone else who I cherish, mean so very much to me.

Watsonville
Saint Patrick's

In 1973 I was ordained a deacon. For those planning to become priests, this is a transitional ministry in the sacrament of holy orders. Some deacons are married and with families and are referred to as permanent deacons because they most likely will not become priests. My assignment was to the historic Saint Patrick's Church in Watsonville. It was a really busy place both night and day. There were three priests as well as myself on the staff: a well-known Irishman from my Dad's home county of Cork, Monsignor Declan Murphy, Max Santamaría from Spain, and John McEvoy, a former Trappist monk somewhat recently come from Ireland. At every evening meal we joked with one another. It was a happy house. Each one of us came from an interesting background and we treasured each one's stories, experiences, and humor. So busy was this place with all the baptisms, the weddings, the *quinceañeras,* and the funerals, not counting the counseling and sacramental preparation classes, that other priests regularly would have to be called in to help in various capacities. For me, this was a good place to learn. Though I felt more and more that I was on *the journey,* I was really being given an opportunity to develop, to expand, *the dream.*

I recall meeting a rather elderly man, perhaps in his late eighties, who was visiting the nearby Saint Francis School taught by the Salesian (S.D.B.) priests and brothers. Someone told me that he was half-Italian and was one of the last of the San Juan Bautista Mission Indians. Whether this description was accurate or not, I am not so sure. But I was very much impressed with him and was then encouraged to find out more about the rich local indigenous and settler history.

That same year saw me attending an ecumenical conference put on by the Episcopal Church at Grace Cathedral in San Francisco. Well known theologians and representatives from the major church traditions presented their findings on the subject of women being ordained to the ministry. Needless to say, it was both provocative and enlightening for me. Nowadays much of that difficult territory has already been explored by many of the churches and they have seen no significant reason to disallow women from service as a deacon, priest, bishop or other minister of the Church. But there are some, my own Church included, who are unable to reach far enough to ordain women to any of the holy orders. I do not think that the issue will easily go away. We will have to let the Holy Spirit be the Holy Spirit to guide us in future decision-making times, I suppose. And we must be open to all future possibilities ("...whatever you permit on earth will be permitted in heaven," Matthew 16: 19).

At this same conference I had the opportunity to spend some time with Brother Roger Schutz, a co-founder of an ecumenical monastery at Taizé which is situated in the middle of France, not so far from St. Bernard's ancient monastic foundation at Cluny. This monastery of Taizé allows its monks to celebrate their Protestant, Catholic, Anglican, or Orthodox way of life and worship as they live as a single community of vowed brothers. Visitors from all over the world note the popularity of its unique multi-language worship music that draws from diverse church traditions. Many of these mantra-like pieces of music are sung locally in both Protestant and Catholic churches. These monks also specialize in working with youth, not only locally, but on an international ecumenical level. Because Brother Roger took the time to give me a special blessing on my future ministry and insisted that I visit Taizé, I have done so and am happy to have done it. Even now I can recall his serene smile as well as his gentle hands placed on my head in blessing.

Deacon Ordination Day, San Carlos Cathedral, Monterey, California, 1973

Life as a Priest

Early Years of Priesthood

On September 7, 1974 I was ordained a priest for the Diocese of Monterey. It was really quite a joyous occasion that will always be imbedded in my memory as long as I shall live. Bagpipe melodies greeted all who entered the church. Guitars and the traditional pipe organ accompanied the songs and hymns of the Mass. It was truly wonderful, and still many years later, I encounter people who were present at the ceremony who recount that it was also an eventful moment in their own lives. Here is a prayer to Jesus that I wrote at the time of my ordination:

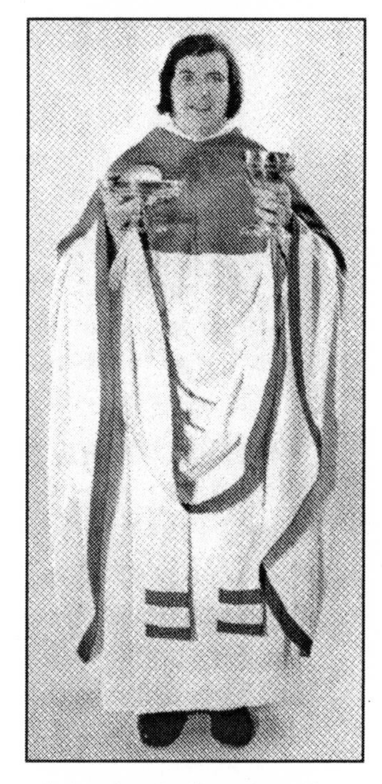

Priestly Ordination Day, September 7, 1974, St. Patrick's Church, Watsonville, California

O Mystery of Mysteries!
You are before me and yet I stand in your presence!
I need You, Lord, more than I have ever needed You before.
I accept your call to extend You in time and space,
to be your hands and your feet and your voice.
I say Yes to what You put before me.
I know more fully that you want all of your brothers and sisters
to be united around your Holy Table.

I believe with all of my heart and mind and soul
that You will give your own strength to me
in the Eucharist of your Love.
As You became human so that we could
ever so gradually share in your divinity,
divinize me with your power and strength
so that I can bring others to You in the assembly of love.
Yes, Lord Jesus,
I have known You for a long time in my short life,
and I am most glad for that singular favor.
When I come daily to your High Feast with my Thanks—Yes, take it
and do with it whatever You will.
For yours are the power and the glory forever! Alleluia!

CAPITOLA
SAINT JOSEPH'S

Celebrating Doctor of Ministry degree

My first assignment as a priest was Saint Joseph's Church in Capitola, serving with its beloved Irish pastor, John Kennedy. I was overjoyed to be there because the church was brand new, fulfilled the liturgical norms of time, and was and continues to be, one beautiful piece of worship architecture: a fitting house in which to assemble the local people of God. Though it took a certain amount of time to become familiar with my priestly duties, everyone was most helpful and understanding. Whatever little or big mistakes that I made were continually forgiven and usually forgotten by most of the parishioners. Both clergy and people of the diocese helped me to flesh out the roles of becoming "strong, loving, and wise..." (Titus 2:2). Here I worked on a second Master's Degree in Liturgy, and then a short time later began to work on a Doctor of Ministry Degree Program put on by the Jesuit School of Theology at Berkeley, California. I received this degree in 1979. It had an ecumenical focus and stressed helping people to make or receive positive change in their local situation. Great for parish work, I thought, and so I went ahead with it. The Krilanovich-Jahnigen family, Gay Howard Pollock, Stuart Carlsen and some other wonderful people were for me an important part of this educational enterprise. The life experiences of each one of these people taught me much about ministry, the act of serving one another in God's name.

A Child Is Born

Early on in my ministry at Saint Joseph's, I was given a most extraordinary experience. As is perhaps common for many priests, ministers, and other professionals who touch the lives of people, certain families and individuals, by their welcoming actions and concern, draw us into closer relationship with them. Though admittedly, one needs to be cautious at times, nonetheless there exist those safe and wholesome folks who reach out to share an extra measure of altruistic hospitality. Such people often become our special friends and abide with us throughout the years of both ministerial service and life.

As often happens to lots of young folk in the course of growing up, one of our high school youth became pregnant. As the family was close-knit, deeply spiritual, and well known to me, they sought my help. I spent some worthwhile time counseling with the family and the young lady herself over the months leading up to the birth of her child. Along the way, they kept mentioning to me that, since I was really a part of their family, I definitely should try to be present in the birthing room at the decisive moment. I was not so sure of my exact role in this part of the helping process; I thought that perhaps I might discreetly be somewhere else far away when news of the moment of birth would come. But it so happened that I was nearby when their call came.

Full of a kind of mysterious excitement and not sure of what was really going to happen, I rushed to the hospital and entered the room, only to be greeted by the young woman's siblings and mother. The doctor was already busy attending to her. Pretty soon the baby came forth and, much to my surprise, the doctor, mistakenly thinking that I was the father (this was not so!), invited me to sever the umbilical cord. I did so with a certain amount of trepidation mixed with joy. What a privilege! I do not believe that this kind of experience is for all of our priests (or even some natural fathers of families), but it was mine and I cherish it. What a miracle Life is! The child born that day, Eric, grew up well, and I have run into him at various times. He always smiles when people remind him of what occurred at my hands.

Then, a short time into my time of being an associate pastor, yet another important event took place that changed my life forever.

A Young Person Enters into Greater Life

One day I was contacted by a Chippewa Cree family who asked me to celebrate the funeral of one of the younger members of the family. It was a really sad time for everyone, I could see. They made it clear that, as Catholics, they also wanted to celebrate Indian ceremonies as well. Not knowing all that this might entail, I agreed to offer help in any way that I could.

As the hours and days leading up to the funeral went by, from a spiritual point of view and with a pastoral heart, I noticed how their own faith sustained them through those most difficult empty moments. They stood united and did the important activities that are always required at such times, gratefully accepting condolences and special kindnesses from their neighbors and friends. Lots of relatives and acquaintances came from Montana, South Dakota, and other parts of California to be with them. I remember the medicine man and his dear wife, the St. Johns, who came from afar to help with the prayers in the tradition of the Peoples of the plains. The ears of the mourners participating in the vigil at the mortuary were filled with the hushed sounds of drum and voices repeating ancient songs. Throughout the night all present were invited to get up and stand before the assembly to share words of comfort and encouragement as they spoke of the family member and friend lying before us. I took my place among them. With a special urge that can only come from the Spirit, I was led to share with them a native song that I had learned how to sing some years before.

The next day the drum and singers were present for the mass of resurrection in the parish church in Capitola. The *wicasa wakan* (medicine man), I believe, was quite surprised, and happily so, when I invited him to share the communion cup with the people as I shared the holy bread. It was my first truly cross-cultural liturgy and, as I sensed it at the time, the beginning of something new for my work. Later, on the anniversary of the death we celebrated a special memorial mass outside in the garden of the family house. The music was a bit less subdued and once again the medicine man helped with communion. All this has been so many years ago, yet it is as clear as day to me now. I look upon this family as my special life-long friends.

Some time later, Mary Riotutar, a respected elder, invited me to a powwow at Cabrillo College in Aptos, just a short distance from where I lived. The family was always involved, I came to discover, in ensuring that Indian events occurred with some measure of regularity within the County of Santa Cruz and places nearby. It was probably my first powwow and it was a wonderful experience. Beginning on a Friday evening, it would continue on until Sunday afternoon.

The first thing that one hears after parking the car is the sound of the drum and voices intoning the songs. It does something special to all who hear it. It is, in reality, the sound of the universal heartbeat, and it beckons all who hear and feel it to come to the circle, the arbor, to dance. It is a metaphor for life itself. Once in the midst of everyone gathered, the sound seems to intensify itself. There one experiences a great harmonious connection; all visitors are caught up in it. One cannot help but to move the feet to the voice of the drum. It is a primeval sound for all human beings, I believe; probably for the animals, birds, and the rest of creation as well.

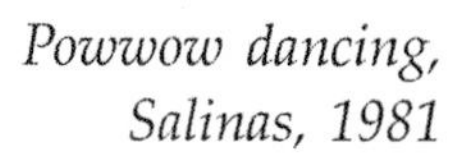

Powwow dancing, Salinas, 1981

Mary, constantly smiling, started introducing me to lots of the elders and other folks connected with putting on the powwow, as well as to plenty of visitors who had come from afar. Even though at first I was shy and thought that everyone was looking at me (and they were!), she took me into the circle to dance along with everyone else. I was not wearing the preferred feathers and beadwork outfit, but I soon began to feel the rhythm and get caught up in the movement and the sound of the drum's backbeat. My first steps may have been stiff and not properly executed, but the beat picked me up and I was able to complete circle after circle, dance song after dance song.

What a wonderful moment in time. I had joined representatives of all the tribes, it seemed, and was enjoying their own particular kind of cultural hospitality. As time went by I got invited to some other nearby powwows and indigenous events. Several were held at the University of California at Santa Cruz, another at the fairgrounds in Watsonville, as well as at the junior college in Salinas. One time I was invited to bless the powwow dance circle and environs in the traditional way with offerings of tobacco and sage and sweetgrass at the Casa de Fruta grounds near Hollister. I might also mention that early on in his role as the new leader of Monterey Diocese, Bishop Sylvester Ryan participated in the opening of a Red Road Sobriety Powwow. I felt it important that he get to know some of his spiritual constituents. He seemed quite overwhelmed, perhaps joyfully overwhelmed, as we all danced together in what is called the "grand entry" which traditionally opens the powwow. I helped to prepare a four directions prayer that he offered on that day. It was well received and he was encouraged to become involved as much with Native concerns as he was able.

My world of Native activity continued to open up, especially at the times when I was called upon to celebrate baptisms, confirmations, weddings and, sadly, funerals. Many are the times that I was asked to offer a prayer over food at special events. Some tribal traditions call for the setting apart of a "spirit plate" to honor the presence of God's invisible creations, the spirits, or as other cultures commonly refer to them, the "angels" who are God's messengers. However the accepted customs were, I always tried to offer a prayer voiced in a form that made sense to anyone within earshot, but especially to Native folks. It has always been a joy for me to do this.

Grand Entry Dance with Bishop Sylvester Ryan, Red Road Sobriety Powwow, Hollister, California, 1993

Whether food blessings at a meal, or larger occasions like weddings or funerals, each time I have tried to include appropriate rituals and ceremonies that honor and respect the traditions of tribes represented at the gathering.

From the late 70s I started noticing more and more Aztec dancers participating at Native events that up until then were usually more "north of the border" in focus. I know that some folks at that time had difficulties with this due to their language and the distinctive regalia (huge plumed feathers, etc.), but as time went by, I know that acceptance has prevailed. Some events were held on the grounds of the old mission in San Juan Bautista. I remember people like Chemo Candelaria and Suni Reyna taking the microphone and giving lengthy instructional talks to those who were present. I believe that, each in their own ways, these people helped further the process of acceptance of "south of the border" native cultures. This was a good and necessary move.

A few times in those days I was invited to bless the feathers and sacred items of the Aztec dancers. Once in a while I would catch some of them staring at me from the corner of their eyes and I would feel them silently wondering, "Who is this White guy who wants to bless our sacred items? Does he really understand what we are about? Should we go ahead and let him do it?" They would look on and sometimes seem a bit mystified. Undauntedly realizing that this was one more opportunity to share spirituality, I always felt that it is better to offer my services, even at the risk of making a mistake, rather than to say or do nothing. I have found that most of us, whenever we can get past the language barriers, and if we want to, can always find ways to connect with each other in sincerity by means of mutual respect and appreciation.

Upon occasion, nearby Aztec groups with the "*palabra*" (the acceptable right to dance and follow the Aztec way) have "prayer-danced" at baptisms, weddings, *quinceañeras* (celebrations for the fifteenth birthday of a Mexican-heritage young woman), funerals, memorials, and special events like anti-gang demonstrations or special colorful parades against neighborhood, *barrio* (neighborhood) violence. Happily, many of these groups are not afraid to dance inside our churches nowadays, once an invitation is given. But a lot of our priests and ministers need to be enlightened, not only about indigenous sacred danced prayer and its meaning, but also concerning Indian ways in general. Yet, as time goes by, I am sure that these things will be normalized.

Numerous times I have received a phone call or answered a knock on my door to pray with or for someone in need. Perhaps many of us have been called upon at times to do so. Invariably, if the person asking were Native, I would be offered symbolic gifts of tobacco or sage wrapped up in red cloth. This is customary when visiting a medicine person or someone known to have a special gift of healing. In themselves they are not usually costly and represent a tiny part of the bounty of Mother Earth. These kinds of items symbolize prayer and appreciation for the one asked to offer the prayer. I continue to receive items like these. I use them for their sacred purposes or I pass them along to others who are in need of them. This is the Native form of gift giving: to appreciate something, to take it in to oneself, and then let it go, often into the hands of other folks so that they too might appreciate it, so that they might draw strength or joy from it.

Santa Cruz
Holy Cross

In 1978 I was assigned to serve in the historic church of Holy Cross, Santa Cruz along with its pastor, Monsignor Michael Buckley and Father Gerry McCormack. Both were quite popular, each for his own style of being a priest. It is a modern parish boasting a white New England-style brick gothic building sitting on the foundations of a mission prepared about two hundred years earlier to serve Native People of the surrounding areas. The Sunday liturgy, indeed, all the worship services, were contemporary, yet based on ancient church practices. People were friendly, and, even though most of the church members felt a special sort of closeness, they were not too "clannish" or "parochial." On the contrary, they always reached out to welcome visitors, whether local or from other countries in the world. Often such visitors would remark to me after Mass how they enjoyed the music and the sense of closeness within the worship assembly. The property also contains a smaller-sized replica of the ancient Spanish-Native mission chapel. I took advantage of an opportunity to refurbish it in order to open it up to more and more for spiritual activities that required a quiet and intimate ambiance. We even made it available for the local Greek Orthodox priest who had no church in which to celebrate Lenten vespers. Now daily mass and special services are held there, I am glad to report.

Enjoying Scottish Games with Patrick Hohmann, Pebble Beach, California, 1980

Here I led numerous weddings and funerals, some of which included elements of Native acculturation. It is easy for me to recall a special wedding in which the couple, Native People from both sides of the border, exchanged eagle feathers along with their rings. Together they covered themselves with a special blanket to symbolize unity and common destiny. Smudging, the burning of sage or cedar or sweetgrass or tobacco, sacred herbs for the People, usually accompanied the ceremonies.

Sad to say, one particular funeral stands out in my mind. It was for a prominent young Lakota woman who perished in a car accident while her newborn child survived. Again, tribal ceremonies were celebrated during the funeral mass. Afterwards, the grieving husband and family asked me to baptize the child. I did so the next day, with most of the same people present and actively participating. In spite of what had preceded it, the ceremony was a joyous event. We even brought forward some of the same blessed water used to sprinkle the mother's coffin the day before. From death to life...: "we have left death and have passed over into life." (1 John 3:14). This is the faith that has always been shared with me from my youth, and this what we celebrated on that momentous occasion. That little girl Waeva grew up into a wonderfully talented young woman. On September 17, 1987 we were all privileged to hear her pray in the Lakota language during the historic Mass of Pope John Paul II at Laguna Seca near Monterey. Dressed in her tribal finery, she represented her People very well, both in word and deed. From death to life to greater life, it seems that faith can carry us very far indeed.

A Spiritual Experience: Vision Questing

It was while I was serving this wonderful church of people that I was invited by some Native friends to fast in the mountains in the traditional Indian way. They taught me how to spend several days alone in the hills without food or water, all the time praying and relying

Hiking in Santa Cruz Mountains, 1980

Hiking in the Scottish Highlands with friend Chris Christie, 1980

on God for personal life-situation clarities that would be revealed. I definitely feel that these clarities, these purposes in life, come to us from a place of divine inspiration. Some call this type of spiritual activity a "vision quest" or "crying for a vision," others simply, "fasting." The experience calls upon the individual to trust the Creator of all, to have self-reliance, and to be close to the actions of Mother Earth: rhythms of the day and night, the weather, sun, moon and stars, birds and animals, beings that fly or crawl, light and dark and the shades in between, as well as all else that exists in the created world, whether visible or invisible. Temporarily forgetting all the everyday affairs of modern living, a person is able to take some time apart with Wakan Tanka, Akbáatadia, Maheo, or, in plain English, God Who Is The Great Mystery Of All Life. I would suggest that there are also other ways to do this; and those folks coming from different religious traditions, I am sure, will find similar methods of doing something spiritually, something that is above and beyond one's usual comfort zone, something communicative with God and the marvelous creation, in order to achieve a greater sense of unity and purpose in one's life. My only caution is to stress how important it is to "check in" with those who have proper knowledge, those uniquely wise individuals who can legitimately guide others, before and after attempting to pursue this sort of quest.

With John Grinnell and bare-footed Rev. Noel King after a wedding, Santa Cruz, California, 1981

With Greek Orthodox priest after a Catholic ordination, 1981

Celebrating part of my culture in Santa Cruz, California, 1981

In Holland, 1982

With my ever-faithful and well-travelled Karmann-Ghia, 1982

I must not forget to mention one rather important person in my life: Noel King. We met while I was helping out as chaplain at the university and we became good friends from the start. At the time he was more of a professor rather than a ministering priest with congregation. Since my youth I have always had a special connection with the Anglican Church ("Episcopal" in the U.S.A.). Perhaps, having been born in London, the center of many things Anglican, at a very early age I became conscious of "the other churches" that were somewhat like us Roman Catholics. As I grew up, I came to learn more and more about our unique ecclesial histories. While in Santa Cruz I started to hear about this renowned professor of religious studies who at one time was voted most popular professor at the school.

We worked together on several kinds of projects with the students as he gradually revealed himself to be one of the most knowledgeable teachers concerning both Islam and Hinduism. Not only a scholar but also an ordained Anglican priest, he seemed to connect well with anyone on a spiritual journey, myself included. I can still remember his smile and wise words as we would sip tea (or something stronger) upon occasion. I sensed that he had a great respect for me, regarding me as an equal, though he was perhaps twice my age. Since he was born in India, his father English and his mother a native of India, he was comfortable in both worlds. At home he could often be found wearing a traditional men's wrap-around skirt so common in the land of his birth. As a tribute to both humility and his heritage, he would celebrate the Holy Eucharist in full vestments minus shoes and socks. People seemed to really like this about him. Simultaneously he stood for both order and "holy disorder." As many of us learn spiritual ways just by being around spiritual people like Noel, we all could take a life lesson from him. Intellectual though he was, he balanced his attributes with humor and did not take himself too seriously. May his gentle spirit live on!

San Luis Obispo
The Old Mission

In 1981 I was assigned to Old Mission San Luis Obispo, ready to help out Fathers Jim Nisbet, Dennis Gilbert, and George McMenamin.

I really did not know what to expect as a group of friends and I drove down Highway 101 with all my worldly belongings in tow. Upon arrival at the church I was told that I was needed immediately to celebrate the 5:30 PM Mass. With little time to properly prepare, I "winged it" and found it to be a good experience. Hundreds of eyes were upon me, scrutinizing my every move during the mass, I felt, but the congregation seemed warm and anxious to meet me. This was how I was received later on by all the folks, and it signaled to me that my stay at this historic- church-active-parish was going to be a fruitful period of time, not only in my personal life, but also in my life of being a priest. *The journey* was continuing *and* I was given more possibilities to experience *the dream*.

Chumash Country

This mission, set up in 1772 in the midst of the Chumash People, was built by them, and was intended to serve them. As the weeks and months gradually went by, various people of Native heritage approached me to chat or to do something for them. Nearby, on the Carissa plains, not far from the little town of Santa Margarita, I once again had some opportunities to meet individuals who made up the Redwind Community, an intertribal intentional commune that had been set up by Grandfather Semu Huaute, a Chumash elder. The first time that I had met these people was in 1973 in the City of Paso Robles where they were doing some kind of public relations work at the downtown park in order to assure the locals, mostly ranching folks, that they meant no harm. They were apparently trying to ward off some future possible Indian/non-Indian prejudicial situations. Though my own schedule did not permit me to be in contact with them very often, I was nevertheless impressed by the whole idea of people going back to the land and living the traditional ways, while at the same time staying in touch with the same kind of world that the rest of us inhabit. In later years, on the last of these visits, I was really saddened to hear that its population had become greatly reduced because many folks feared the danger of the uranium deposits slipping into, and in a foul manner already polluting, the natural waters that they had depended upon for their daily existence.

New Friends

One day an exhibition of some kind was being held in the plaza area outside the front doors of the church. There were a lot of booths containing various literatures concerning different groups like the girl and boy scouts, political and environmental groups, etc. As I passed by a particular display, my eyes focused on a special Indian exhibit. I also noticed that the exhibitor was wearing some authentic-looking Native clothing. We talked about what he was showing everyone and came to realize that we had many things in common. It was the beginning of a good friendship. This young man, Ed Jensen, knew many of the local Indian People and was dedicated, along with his then-girlfriend-now-wife Sara, to the work of replicating and designing Indian items according to the old authentic ways. Sara, I came to discover, always had a special love for the designs of the Peoples of the Plateau (Nez Percé, Umatilla, Cayuse, etc.), while Ed felt close to the Plains Peoples (Lakota, Cheyenne, Crow, etc.). Ed invited me to a few gatherings, both powwows and other kinds. One day we had a sweat lodge ceremony on a ranch nearby followed afterwards by a sumptuous meal especially prepared by Sara. Over the years I have visited Ed and Sara and their family in Idaho Falls, Idaho. I look upon both of them as, not only friends, but as special consultants on native culture. They are detail specialists in every way. And, like me, their lives have been much enlarged by the traditions and spirituality of Native People. It is always helpful to know that on *the journey* there are others who share *the dream*.

Tradition

At San Luis Obispo I learned about some of the drum songs of the Chumash People that many years earlier had been "translated" and then transferred into the sounds of the historic mission bells. Daily, as the bells ring out, passersby and folks further away can hear both transformed ancient native rhythms as well as Spanish rhythms used to announce the special hours of the day and festive moments in life like baptisms, weddings, and funerals. Most tourists and locals and most of our priests, I am sure, are not even aware of this ancient

My tenth anniversary of ordination celebration,
Scotts Valley, California 1984

Bagpipers at farewell mass, Mission San Luis Obispo, 1983

heritage. Happily, the parish continues its traditions of teaching new bell ringers some of these melodies. In more recent years I have come to know John Warren, a fine musician and choral leader in the San Luis County area who, with his New World Orchestra and Singers, promotes ancient California Mission music, wonderful pieces that are both Spanish and ethnically Chumash or Salinan in heritage.

It is good to see the old ways like those just mentioned continuing on yet enfolded in so many contemporary expressions. Perhaps this is what "Tradition" is all about. Tradition, with a "capital T," is really made up of many "small t" traditions. From generation to generation, numerous little traditions become woven together to make up a particular tribe's traditional heritage, the heritage that perhaps outsiders see as most prominent. But closer inspection will reveal the necessity of these less visible traditions. For example, I suppose that it is as if the myriads of varieties of inherited family and restaurant recipes for pasta, now so international and ubiquitous, come together to describe that wonderful dish we call "spaghetti." Like these recipes, somehow each indigenous tradition, unique though it may be and special as it is lived out, contributes to the fullness of Native culture and practice. For that matter, the same could be said about any culture as well.

Bishop Thaddeus Shubsda processing with mitre and cope vestments I made for Holy Year ceremony, San Luis Obispo, California, 1982

I learned long ago that tradition is not just wearing something old, like your grandparent's hat. Nor is it traipsing something out of a museum cabinet for a little "show and tell." It is really about doing something ancient, but in a new and fresh way, like … having a baby. The ancient pattern becomes freshly expressed in a particular moment of revelation. I wonder what little traditions and ways of doing things in our families and among our friends, or life habits that each of us has created, will actually be carried on into the future of our common humanity. Perhaps now is a good time for each one of us to reflect upon what is really that important enough to pass on to the next generations. Mmm! Here is some food for thought.

Artichokeland: First Pastorate: Castroville

In 1983 the Parish of Our Lady of Refuge in Castroville needed a new pastor. I decided to take on that role. At that time and for many years before, the primary industry was and continues to be the growing of artichokes. Though the church is located in the town itself, the parish geography covers a large area of, not only Castroville, but also Oak Hills, Moss Landing, Prunedale, as well as the edges of the constantly growing City of Salinas. Each section has its own uniqueness, yet all claim the church as their own. The parishioners now as then are Mexican immigrants, Mexican Americans, Swiss-Italians, Filipinos, military families, along with many others of various ethnic backgrounds. The primary languages needed at any moment are English and Spanish. I assessed, as many new pastors of my time were to do, that I had arrived at a time when lots of things

Shortly after arriving at new assignment as pastor in Castroville, California, 1983

A pastor glad to serve the people, Castroville, 1987

within the parish community and the community at large were in need of change of one kind or another. I tried to facilitate that change, though I must admit, it was not so easy to coalesce vastly different communities of people, each with their own principles, unique heritages, religious standards, different languages, and ... varying degrees of a stubbornness, the kind of endemic obstinacy that fails to allow individuals to focus together on a larger picture of what could make a parish better for everyone. As is quite understandable, some folks were quite content to dwell in their own particular comfort zones, whether that zone had to do with age, culture, devotional custom or received religious tradition, etc. The sense of religious belonging was not so homogeneous. Nor was everyone used to thinking pastorally about the "whole parish." It is a common difficulty for many spiritual leaders, Christian or other, I think. But, as they say, change was on the way. I believe that I tried to bring positive change to benefit everyone in that particular setting not so long ago. After all, I thought at the time, I have been specially trained to be an agent of positive change in the communities in which I would live. But in all humility, I must say that I was simply one more person with a pastoral heart who was taking my place in the long line of others who had served and who will come to serve in any particular church setting. I have been told repeatedly that my work there was not in vain because they still talk about me positively. I am always glad to hear this. At times I return to help out with weekend services and weddings and funerals.

Though the daily work was really challenging, many wonderful adventures awaited me in this parish in relation to Indian People. First of all, I came to know individuals who were from the Ohlone Tribe, scattered as they are throughout this part of California. One would introduce me to another and so on. I especially remember Robert Martin, a bearded elder of many years who shared with me that he was born in the hills above the not so far away town of Aptos about eighty years before. My imagination would activate as I wondered how the lay of the land was at that time. Where were Indian families actually living? By the streams, or were their villages near the beach? What work was available to them in those days? What particular aspects of their unique culture would they be able to celebrate and pass on in the quickly changing world by which they were surrounded? Many questions came to my mind.

Using for a blessing rite an artichoke grown in nearby fields by Castroville parishioners

One day some of us were remodeling the side chapel of the church in order to make it more available for different kinds of gatherings: Mass, bible study, religious education classes for the children, meditation, etc. With a growing youth population, gathering space was at a premium in those days. I was standing on a ladder rearranging the framed Stations of the Cross when Robert Martin appeared with another elder, Patrick Orozco, a well-respected Ohlone leader from Watsonville. After sharing with me some of his family background, he asked how he could peruse some ancient church baptismal records in order to verify his family genealogy. I felt good that I was asked to assist. The meeting led to my getting to know many other Ohlone families who felt themselves historically connected with their ancestors through several of the Spanish missions that are within our diocese.

These people of the acorn and the abalone birthright helped me to notice "the lay of the land" from their perspectives as well: the special significance of the local mountains, the ocean, the trees, birds and animals, the cloud formations, and even the sites of ancient, now vanished, villages. As I got more involved in the work of the parish and diocese, I came to know individuals and families of other tribes: Esselens, Navajos, Lakotas, Blackfeet, Kiowas, Apaches, Kickapoos, Pomos, not to mention folks whose Native heritages are from south of our national border.

Stressed out with too much church work! Need to go travel! 1985

Vacations

I usually travelled to Europe on most of my summer vacations. After spending some time (not really enough "quality" time with them, they would always remind me!) with my relatives in different sections of Britain and Ireland, I would then go on the Continent and explore countries whose spoken languages were Italian, French, German, Dutch, or Spanish. Each time I would always look for the least expensive charter flight that would land in the most convenient European airport to allow me the maximum advantage in utilizing my Eurail Pass for train travel. Each year someone different would travel with me, my only requirements being that they were not to be boring and needed to be able to handle a trip of several weeks, each day allowing themselves to meet new people, and also see a new country every day or so. Our many adventures would require me to write another book, so I will await that opportunity. Perhaps I only saw and experienced a Europe that I felt was contemporary back then, twenty or so years ago. We know that it has changed drastically over the last few years, especially since our recent wars. But meanwhile, I thank God for the invention of photographs that help recall some of my memories.

Just can't quite make it to the next mountain peak, the Sierras, California

After being in Castroville for a year or so I met a young man from Caracas, Venezuela, who really impressed me and everyone else around with his infectious enthusiasm, wonderful singing voice and great skill with the guitar and, for his young age at the time, depth of spirituality. He carries an appellation that one does not easily forget: Igor Simonóvis. He had wanted to become a Franciscan in California, but soon gave it up with the idea of returning home to think things over. He needed a few weeks to "hang out" before heading south once again. At his request I offered him hospitality at my parish home. Lucky for me, he insisted on helping me with any Spanish-language activities in the parish. I could not resist his offer because at the time I was struggling in my Spanish language ability and rather badly needed a helper in the parish.

Igor was that special boost the parish needed. Being already trilingual (Spanish, Italian, and some English), he took it upon himself to transform the music at the masses, bringing in some of those wonderful rhythmic melodies from his own country. The youth flocked to him and a group was formed. All ages were touched by him. His openness to change and his deep compassion for all people was evident to me. I saw in him a future priest. Then and there I decided to do all I could to encourage him in his call.

As time went by he was able to reconsider things sufficiently so as to put himself on the path of a vocation to serve once more; and he did. After a circuitous route that took him from Castroville to Venezuela to Italy, he now serves as a founder of a new order of brothers in the Ukraine. I feel that I was once a part of his formation and rejoice with him in his sacred work. I am sure that now he is proficient in other languages as well.

I thank Igor for inviting me so many years ago to visit his home and friends in Venezuela. My Dad joined me on that wonderful trip. It gave him an opportunity to relive his youth very well. The spirit of adventure was still inside him. I can still envision him lying on the beach at Cata near Caracas, with all the pretty girls in bikinis attending to him; or inspecting banana trees on the edge of the jungle, or even struggling to breathe in the thin air of Pico Bolivar in the Andes Mountains near Mérida. I can see him being frustrated at not being able to express himself fully at dinners and parties when there was no trusty interpreter nearby, or the back pain that troubled him for days after he flipped out of his hammock, hitting the cement hard. Thank God that Igor's friend, Osman Salamanca, was there to comfort Dad, massaging his back into full recovery, both of them chatting in broken German and English throughout. That first trip to South America prepared me for the many other travel experiences that were to happen in my life. I had responded positively to someone's invitation and I am the better for it.

After a few years, I found it alluring, and later enjoyable, to go "out West," to see what I had not yet seen, to experience that which I had only heard of or read about in books. Besides, I always liked to drive, to see the wonders of nature, and to allow myself to reflect on what was going on in my life at the time. Here now was a new way to experience *the journey* guided by *the* ancient *dreams* that I held within my person.

While on vacation one summer many years ago, perhaps in 1985, I met a wonderful couple, Ron and Toni Bird and their extended family. It was, as it seems to be always for me, a chance meeting that occurred on a Friday night at a supper club bar called the Winner's Circle in Cutbank, Montana. It was a noisy, but welcoming place. The rock music was excellent and there was a lot of dancing. I was really enjoying myself, "Montana-style," I thought. The tables and chairs were very close to each other and somehow through the conversation Ron found out that I was a priest, even though I was trying to be a bit low profile about it. We talked a lot and when it was time to leave, he and Toni graciously invited us to spend the night at their house on the reservation in lieu of us camping out in the cold. We immediately accepted the offer. I remember that Ron and his friends kept us up most of the night telling us Indian-Whiteman jokes. It was a lot of fun, even though I realized that the Whiteman was the butt of the joke every time! Here was my introduction to Indian humor, I suppose. We also talked about our families and some of our life experiences and grew very tired after a while due to all the traveling and the dancing that we had done. Finally we all went to sleep.

The next morning the most wonderful fragrance of home-cooked bacon and that great aroma of morning coffee woke us. After cleaning up we went down for breakfast. What a surprise! I did not know that Ron and Toni had invited most of their family from

Surrounded by the lakes and Rocky Mountains so dear to the Blackfeet Tribe of Montana

nearby to meet us and have breakfast with us. What a spread it was! It took about three hours to finish the meal because there was so much food and conversation. When it was near the end I was asked to bless the house, which I gratefully did and we went on our way, but not before receiving some great advice concerning the best way for us to travel so that we would see many interesting places as we headed for the Canadian border through the Blackfeet Reservation. It was well worth it, for we experienced breathtaking mountain vistas, shining lakes and rivers, and were privileged to see the famous Bighorn sheep of the Rocky Mountains. The eternal, serene beauty of the Rocky Mountains continues to amaze me to this day.

These most generous people stayed in contact with me and later on that year invited me to come back for an extended visit. I have returned many times, not only learning firsthand something about Blackfeet history, culture, and hospitality through their family and friends, but also by participating in North American Indian Days, the great powwow that the tribe sponsors each year. There I have had enjoyable times dancing in the arbor with everyone else, visiting in teepees, their temporary traditional homes, helping to make and sell fry bread, and celebrating Mass and a baptism in the Blackfeet way, complete with dance, traditional headdresses and outfits, and this People's own language spoken in the prayers. My share in *the journeying* was continuing, supported by *the dreams* that I was having. I was beginning to recognize much more clearly some of my unfolding destiny, not only as a parish priest in general, but as one who also was connecting with Native People. And it felt good.

For quite a few summers I took it upon myself to explore some places in "Indian country" that I had not yet visited, from California on up to Washington State and across Idaho to Montana and the Dakotas. Each time God revealed to me something more of the world of Native Peoples. At the same time I became further acquainted with some of the important cities in surrounding states, as well as the uncountable smaller towns scattered all over a particular state's terrain. There is just so much to see and explore, especially when one leaves the interstate and other main roads. One then meets the most wonderful people. By making new friends, and staying in contact with them, my life has become full indeed. Friendship is such a gift. Often it is serendipitous. We usually do not know ahead of time who we will accept into our lives as a friend, or who will choose to befriend us. It just seems to happen. Some friends are for life, others are with us for only a short time. We treat best friends in a special way, while at the same time relating to many others. Trust is involved, we know, but so are loyalty and concern. Some of us make friends easily, while others take a long time to develop closeness. Perhaps a lot has to do with our early childhood and how we have been formed. Or perhaps the ease with which we make friends has to do with how we have overcome betrayal in the past with forgiveness and hope. Friendship is something of a mystery to me. But I love to explore it and share in it. Friendship is *the journey* that allows *the* many new and fantastic *dreams* of our lives to become realized in all of us.

During some of these summer breaks while travelling around the country, I had opportunities to participate in many Tekakwitha Conferences. Each time the tribal peoples of that year's particular area would host the event by sharing their own particular ceremonies and traditions with participants from far away. Much of the day's activities would include talks, small group meetings,

Lakota Priest Collins "CP" Jordan (Cetan Luta—"Red Hawk"), a good friend and spiritual advisor

native-way prayer, and numerous other opportunities to meet new people. Always, on the Saturday evening, we would put on a small powwow when everyone came out in brightly colored finery to dance and have a good time. New friendships would inevitably be made, I am sure.

At these conferences I invariably met remarkable women and men, some of whom, like Bobby Geronimo, are descendents of known historic personages like the Apache leader Geronimo or the Lakota warrior Red Cloud. One elder named Collins "CP" Jordan happened to be a recently ordained Catholic priest from the Rapid City Diocese in South Dakota. He spoke fluent Lakota and had been responsible for some translations of the Mass in his own language. His ancestors were the famous warriors Spotted Tail and Red Cloud. Though up in age, he was lively and always ready for a good meal and fun. Several times he was my guest in Castroville and Carmel Valley, becoming good friends with my parents and some of the parishioners. For me, he was a whole world of knowledge and experience contained in a very short body. Everyone who met him was impressed by his ways. He

Powwow, Tekakwitha Conference, Albuquerque, New Mexico, 1996

was constantly thinking of his People, especially the less fortunate ones and was always known to pass on to others in need whatever gifts, monetary or other, that he happened to receive. His fine reputation among the Lakota was celebratory. Earlier on he had been a basketball coach, especially working with teenage girls. He helped people to grow as well as grow up through the sport. Lakotas and many other people that I had met from time to time were pleasantly surprised to know that this basketball enthusiast and encourager of young people had gone on to become an ordained Catholic priest. Now he coaches a celestial team.

Visit of Pope John Paul II to Monterey

September 17, 1987 was a special day for everyone in the Diocese of Monterey because Pope John Paul II came to celebrate a festive Mass at Laguna Seca. Thousands saw him in person as they sat on the hillsides and millions of others related to what was going via television. I was part of the committee which over the previous year began to prepare the liturgy and services. We held auditions in my church for those who were to be the readers and I helped with the judging. Like others, I really felt proud to be part of it all. In our planning we had to take into account not just what was to go on minute by minute, but rather what was to occur second by second. It was quite a task. I composed the intercessory prayers and helped choose and practice the lectors. A few days before the actual event I was informed that I was to be up on the altar near the Pope. "Wow, I didn't expect this!" I thought. Not only was I to guide the readers and intercessors to the microphone, but I was to lead up a special delegation of people from each of our parishes and be the first to receive communion from the Pope's hands. I can still see his face scrutinizing me the moment before he offered me Holy Communion. "Will he insist on putting the holy bread on my tongue (the traditional custom) or will he place it in my hand (our more contemporary practice)?" I asked myself. After all, this was also a kind of "teachable moment" for those watching from near and far. Reluctant or not, to my great relief, he placed it in my hand, the way I was hoping for. What a special day! I really felt that this part of *the journey* was an unfolding of an unexpected *dream*.

Escorting Pope John Paul II back to altar after distribution of communion, Laguna Seca

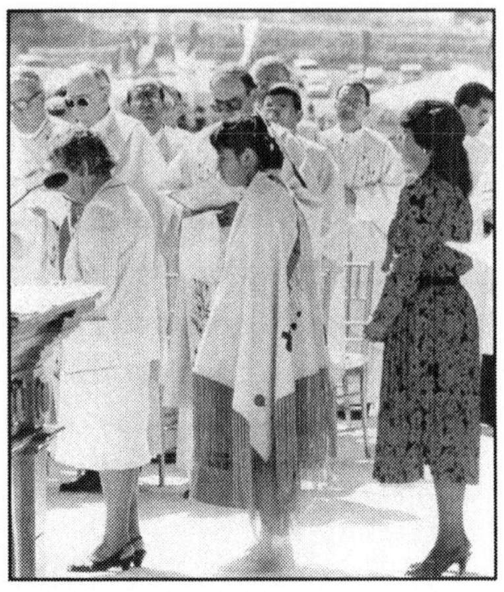

Waeva Gatlin ready to offer prayer in Lakota at Papal Mass, Laguna Seca, near Monterey, California, Sept. 17, 1987

Receiving holy communion from Pope John Paul II, Laguna Seca

I might add that during the previous planning period I had suggested that from the altar area the pontiff should walk down the long ramp and sprinkle the people towards the four directions, in the form of a cross, with an olive branch dipped in holy water. Though, at the rehearsal the day before we were advised to minimize this activity due to time constraints, I suggested to the deacon leading the pope that he just go ahead and follow the original plan. He did so, and both pope and people seemed to really enjoy this special blessing. At that moment, little did many of the assembled folks on the hillside realize that, for Native People, he was also ritually honoring the four directions, calling in the blessings of Creator and sending out prayers for every one and every thing. To this day, I meet individuals who remind me of the joy of that gathering and how blessed they still feel.

Indian People were well represented during this most festive Eucharist in prayers led by Waeva Gatlin, a young Lakota-Chippewa teenager resplendent in an outfit complete with a colorful fringed shawl and an eagle feather properly placed in her hair. She spoke clearly and respectfully in the Lakota tongue. Time seemed to stand still for many of us as she spoke, the sound of her voice echoing across the hillsides. Other Natives were among those who brought special gifts to this impressive world spiritual leader. Friends still remind me of that day. I know that many other proud Indian folks were present in the multitude that sat on the hillside. What a day it was for all of us!

Kateri Circle

My pastoral heart recognized that it was time to start a Kateri Circle, a local gathering of Native People to share fun, food, and faith. It was always open to anyone who identified with her or his Indian heritage. At first, some folks were a bit wary, but by means of the "moccasin telegraph" they came to realize that it would be a good thing for them. So eager were they to be part of it that the meetings grew from once a month to weekly gatherings. Prayer in the presence of burning sage or sweetgrass would open up and close the time together. As various tribes were represented, a wonderful variety of discussion and activity always occurred. Sometimes they would relate about "back home on the rez," the reservation, where many family members still lived, or discuss someone's particular struggle with life. We would all listen patiently as each one shared and then suggestions would be offered. Some of the Kateri Circle members even formed a Native American Alcoholics Anonymous group that met on the church property prior to them participating in our regular meeting. Sometimes we would work on crafts. At other times a few in the group would participate in a weekly sweat lodge ceremony, the leadership of which alternated among those of us who had the right to lead this ancient form of prayer for purification.

One time, a member told us that some unauthorized person, a non-Native, was going to lead a pipe ceremony at a "new age" bookshop nearby in Carmel a few days hence. Supposedly, there was to be a fee involved with the ceremony. We all knew that one must never try to sell spiritual ceremonies. They then made plans to shut this person down. I chuckled a bit at their daring and candor, realizing that such an ethical powerhouse was right here in front of me; but I really agreed with what they wanted to do.

One Navajo friend, Blaine Lucero, was really knowledgeable concerning his own tribe's ceremonial ways and we had many discussions. I learned from him and, I suppose, it was also vice versa. For instance, one morning, he chastised me for leaving out on a table some hawk feathers that I had been cleaning and preparing for ceremonial use. Having worked with them late into the night and, as I was finally ready to go to sleep, I left them neat and in order on the table so that I might finish them up in the morning. Evidently Blaine had seen them lying there when he came in and thought that I was not respecting them properly "in the Indian way." I protested that I was not yet finished with them, but he just walked away in silence. Later on, many hours later that night, he came to my room and apologized for his behavior, saying that Creator had let him know he was to learn many things from me, and that he was sent to "walk in my footsteps," as he put it. I have often reflected on that moment and I recognize it as one more verification sign that I should continue to learn more of the Native ways in order to become more useful as a bridge builder among our many cultures.

Our Kateri Circle members participated in many powwows. We even purchased our own teepee to put up on special occasions.

Once, with the special help of Juan Mancias, our diocesan youth and young adult director who himself is a Kickapoo, we held a "Spiritual Day in Honor of Blessed Kateri Tekakwitha." It took place on the lawn area between the church building and the parish house. A lot of folks showed up, as well as the local Mexican townspeople who were wondering what all the drum sounds echoing in the neighborhood were all about. Drumming, singing, dancing, and lots of fry bread, a powwow staple, were our gifts to everyone who came. It was a good day to remember.

Another time we took on a more reflective spiritual attitude as we gathered together one particular Saturday. We wanted to grow together with a truly Native approach to our Catholic faith. So we invited Father John Hascall from Michigan to help us with the day. A Capuchin Franciscan priest as well as an Ojibwa medicine person, he shared with us many personal stories and reflections. More of this special human being was gradually revealed to us through his healing medicines, like eagle feathers, etc. It was a good day for everyone. He answered many deep questions that folks had and did some healing work. Later on we feasted on traditional foods like salmon, buffalo, deer meat, chokecherries, and the like. I would never erase from my memory such an extraordinary day.

A Special Guest

For a number of months I was able to offer my home for the recovery of Jeremy Two Feathers, a young Lakota who had fallen on hard times and almost lost the use of his leg due to a major infection. As he had no place but the streets of Santa Cruz to recover when he left the hospital, I was glad to make space for him at the rectory in the room next to the kitchen. My dog Dugan was his ever-faithful silent comforter as he slowly healed and got back the partial use of his leg.

As the days and weeks and months of gradual recuperation went by he changed from being quite demanding to actually wanting to listen and really help other people. When he was feeling good he would make beadwork items as little gifts for some of the young people who visited him. He evidently had had a difficult early life, became adopted by a White family far away from his place of birth, and tried to make it on his own at too early an age, at a time when he was least prepared. He told us many amazing stories, but we all knew that alcohol and homelessness had caught up with him. As he got healthier we had many conversations about his past. I was happily surprised to receive letters and a phone call from one of his adopted sisters. They ultimately came out to see him and have remained in touch. They helped me to witness Jeremy finally meet up after many years with his real mother a short time before she died. I am glad that God helped me to be instrumental in helping his life to go better for him. I have seen him several times lately and he is doing well, thanks be to God.

1989 Earthquake

In 1989 an earthquake hit our part of California. Luckily, our church edifice suffered minor damage. A few statues tilted a little, but we were safe. Shortly after it struck, Blaine Lucero, one of our Navajo brothers, recruited us to form an outreach program for donations of food and clothing. He used his expertise to get on the phone to alert many people as to the needs at hand. I remember that after we had gathered lots of supplies, we celebrated in the church a special multicultural blessing ceremony over the donations before they were distributed to those in need. Much of it was expressed through native ritual. It was really touching and inspired many people to be both helpful and hopeful.

Some of the clothing and food items came to be left over after the local earthquake needs were more or less taken care of. As some originally had been earmarked for Native families, Juan Mancias and I placed the excess goods in a trailer, along with a used organ from Holy Cross Church in Santa Cruz and some other items, and we headed for the Crow Reservation in Montana. It took us about eighteen hours of continuous driving, if I recall correctly.

The gifts were well received on the reservation at the village of Pryor, but I was quite taken aback when the reservation parish priest at the time mentioned in passing that the Crows would be really glad to share the large bags of oatmeal with their horses! I knew that the Crow People are fine horsemen, and have been for almost two hundred years, but I thought that they would rather want it for their own families. I, of course, as a "double Celt," had grown up with the many uses of oatmeal, or porridge, as it is called elsewhere across the Atlantic Ocean. Oh well, one more bit of Indian information that I was not privy to beforehand!

Crow Adoption Preliminaries

That trip to Montana after the earthquake turned out to be an eventful one for me. Let me explain. Somehow that same evening after delivering the food and clothes and the organ, I managed to get our truck stuck in a between-the-fields driveway on our way to visit the home of Ervin and Sara Stuart, a couple that I had met the previous summer. I had not known that the local farmer leasing their lands was in the process of irrigating those fields and lots of the water had flowed onto the earthen driveway, making it impassable for us. It was dark and we were tired from driving. "What a mess we are in. How embarrassing for me. People know me around here," I thought.

I got out of the truck, walked up to their house and knocked on the door. Luckily they were home and invited us in. After a quick greeting, I got to the point: we were stuck in the mud. Immediately Ervin brought down his truck and pulled us out to dry land, thanks be to God. We then went back to the house to visit and ate a good meal with them. But then, I was then really surprised to hear Sara uttering these words: "Father Scott, the next time you come up here, we are going to adopt you in our family as a Crow, okay?"

I was at a loss for words. I knew what she meant. Crow People do not take adoption lightly. It is part of their ancient culture and helps to maintain the compact unity of their tribe throughout time and as they experience difficult circumstances. I agreed to the proposal, and after a little more time of visiting, we returned to California. I had a sense that shortly they would make a plan to carry out the adoption at some auspicious time, perhaps in August during Crow Fair, the principal public tribal event for the Crows. Sure enough, that is what happened. Early one evening at the family campsite, in the midst of tribal elders and the extended family and friends (along with a visiting German camera crew filming the ceremony live for their TV station and some Smithsonian Institution volunteers who were studying contemporary Crow tribal culture), I became part of the family, receiving the name *Agisedeh Xiasauch*, Outstanding Warrior. For me, it seemed that *the journey and the dream* were coming together even more.

Lakota Friends

Many years back one of the priests visiting from Ireland who was helping out in the Santa Cruz parish heard that I was involved with Indian People. He referred a couple, Ken One Feather and his wife, to me for a little outreach help. We eventually became friends. They gave birth to a little boy and asked me to baptize him. Immediately upon coming out of the water, the child began to dance excitedly, flinging his feet back and forth in what seemed to be a recognizable Indian dance step. We all saw this as a good omen. On that occasion Ken's brother Smiley had driven down from South Dakota with his wife. After the ceremony they presented me with a *cannupa*, a sacred pipe. I am proud to be a carrier of this pipe and many times have prayed with it along with others. I know of its sacred power. A couple of years after the baptism I had an occasion to visit St. Francis Mission on the Rosebud Reservation, South Dakota. I tracked down Smiley just to say hello. Later he volunteered to help me make a difficult repair on the rental car that I was using. He saved me a lot of money at the time. In many ways I am grateful to many such Lakota People that I have known for their deep sense of spiritual values and their desire to share their goodness with me in hundreds of ways. *Pila maya*, thank you.

Back in the late summer of 1986 I was driving home from a trip to Toronto, the stomping grounds of part of my younger days. I decided to take my time so that I could visit a number of interesting historic places that I had only read about in books. When I reached South Dakota, I stopped by to visit Wounded Knee on the Pine Ridge Reservation. As a fellow priest I thought that it would be good to pay a little visit to the local Jesuit community serving the Lakotas. My colleagues offered me hospitality for the night, also inviting me to help with the following day's powwow Mass. What an experience it was. I had been told, that going back to the early 1880's, about forty percent of the Lakotas are now Episcopalian, another forty percent are Roman Catholic, and the rest claim another denomination or follow only the traditional Lakota religion. Most of the families are *tiospaye,* historically related to one another by blood or marriage.

That powwow mass was a wonderful experience of ecumenical cooperation. Though Roman Catholics and Episcopalians are very close in history and doctrine, there are some significant differences that set us apart. Perhaps many of these differences are resolvable as time goes by. But in the meantime both churches try to work together in common causes, along with other denominational groups. Sometimes this cooperation expresses itself in ingenious ways, and not all of these ways follow official rubrics. For instance, at that particular powwow Mass I saw that there were two altar tables placed together, about an inch apart, so that from a short distance away they appeared to be a single altar. During the worship service some of the usual ritual sacramental actions were shared, while others were time-coordinated. That is, though the priests were in reality standing at separate altar tables and were praying from somewhat similar official prayer texts, the timing of the lifting up of the bread and cup were simultaneous, as were the ritual bowing and genuflection postures.

The assembled worshippers saw what was happening, understood the need for it, and when the moment came to approach for communion, they made the choice to go to their own ecclesial altar table to receive the sacrament. Lakota and English were alternated in the liturgy and the music was both common hymns as well as Lakota *olowan,* Lakota songs. The homily was shared and spoken bilingually. I was asked to offer the closing prayer. At the time it seemed like a wonderful temporary solution to a difficult ecumenical hurdle: a common celebration of the Holy Eucharist. I left the reservation with much to ponder.

Several years later, while still pastor in Castroville, I received letters from the Jesuit superior on the Pine Ridge Reservation asking me to consider spending some time there preparing some men to become permanent deacons. The Jesuit presence on the reservation was to surely become less secure due to the shortage of priestly vocations, he felt, and he was hoping that a good number of traditional Lakota men would go on, after special theological and spiritual formation, to become ordained deacons. As life-long deacons of the

Church, they would be able to care for their local parish communities scattered across the reservation while at the same time also celebrating their "Lakota-ness" in the accepted ancient ways. As spouses and as fathers of their families they would, no doubt, continue what they were already good at: living out the sacrament of marriage. The offer was tempting, but I knew that my bishop at the time, Thaddeus Shubsda, would probably not let me go. Sadly, I had to say no.

New Crow Friends

Another leisurely day's travel took me to Billings, Montana. When I arrived it was oppressively hot and I became caught up in the rush hour traffic. I decided not to stay in the city, consulted my map, found a place called Crow Agency and decided to go there.

The first Crow that I met was Pete Chiefchild, a hitchhiker at the freeway entrance in the direction of the reservation. He is still my friend to this time, for on that day I took a chance and picked him up. He was on his way home to Crow Agency after a rodeo event. I remember that he seemed a bit surprised to hear that I was headed there as well. After about an hour of driving and good conversation, we arrived at his brother's house. Immediately he introduced me to Maria, his sister-in-law, and a bit later to Preston. We enjoyed a cup of tea outside their home and chatted a bit. At the time I felt that this kind of hospitality was a good introduction for me to Crow life. Pete then showed me a good location to camp for the night.

The place had an interesting ambiance. Not only were horses and dogs roaming free in the grassy areas and among the cottonwood trees, but also across the field from me I could see a huge circus-looking tent that at the moment was being used for an evangelical camp meeting. Throughout the night the loudspeakers boomed music and sermons to all within hearing distance. Exhausted from travel, I went to sleep right away, constantly surrounded by such noisy spiritual harangues alternated with folksy hymns accompanied by a country western / rock band. Though on this part of *the journey* I needed a good rest, my sleeping *dream* life surely must have been affected by such goings on as well, I am sure!

The next day Pete brought coffee to wake me up and we breakfasted nearby. Crow Fair had just ended the day before, so there was not much for me to see except a few isolated teepees and stragglers in the campsite area. But he insisted that I come back for it the following summer. During breakfast I found out that he was planning to try his luck at winning some money by entering a rodeo in Cody, Wyoming. When he told me that he was going to hitchhike there, I straight away picked up my map, found where the town was, and, realizing that I had some extra time on my hands, offered to drive him there. Delighted, he threw his bronc saddle and 10-speed bike into the back of my van and we took off.

We journeyed through the bottom part of the reservation and on roads that probably had never before seen tourists. All the way to his destination he proudly spoke about his family and the distinctiveness of Crow culture. It was a great day of learning for me, as well as the beginning of a new friendship. Because we stayed in touch that year I did indeed return the next August for Crow Fair. But the getting to Crow Fair itself has its own special story.

As soon as I had arrived in Montana that next summer, my VW van motor gave up the ghost just outside of Livingstone, about half a day's journey away from the start of Crow Fair. I was so devastated and wondered what I should do? The local car mechanic said that it would be about a week more until the car would be ready. Not having much choice, I said: "Go ahead, fix it." Having said this, I set out on foot to explore the town and look for a motel. I happened to pass by the nearby Catholic Church where the housekeeper listened to my story of woe. Though she was grieving from the recent loss of her brother, she lovingly took the time to suggest that I call the cathedral in Billings to ask for the help of a Crow parishioner who just might take me to the reservation. I did so, and it worked. "God works in wonderful, mysterious ways, even here in Montana!" I thought.

Pete Chiefchild, Crow, holding a roadkill porcupine, Montana 1986

Taking the next greyhound bus for Billings, I was met on my arrival by a generous couple who later were to bring me into their family circle: Norman and Angeline Whiteman, two bilingual Crow Catholics who resided in Billings but who also had a house on the reservation. That Norman was a Notre Dame Football Team fan I could recognize from his cap. Angie was a volunteer in various parish and diocesan ministries. They worked it out so that, after taking me to the pow-wow grounds, I got to stay at the priest's house in "Crow," as the locals affectionately called the town of Crow Agency.

It was the best thing that could happen to me. Here I met a lot of people informally, not only Crows themselves, but also Father Charlie Robinson O.F.M.Cap., the pastor of Saint Dennis Church. His gentle mannerisms, pastoral expertise, and great knowledge of the Crows have really helped me to grow in respect and appreciation for this great tribe. He introduced me to many friends who, over the years, have furthered my own experiences with Native culture. I owe much to this man's great sense of spirituality. He is as generous as is his memorable smile.

I have gone back to Crow Country many times over the years. It is my second home, especially since I came to be adopted and have family and good friends living in different parts of the reservation and elsewhere as well. As a priest, but also as a friend, I have been given numerous opportunities to celebrate *Apsaaloke* (Crow) baptisms, weddings, funerals, as well as times of special prayer. I have participated in a great number of sweat lodge ceremonies, the opening of the sacred bundles ritual, Sundance preparations, vision quest, and the annual parade dance. Both the Crow People and their priests and medicine persons have helped to integrate me into their own unique experience of life. I am most grateful to all of them for this special gift.

Norman and Angeline Whiteman, Father's Crow relatives

Sabbatical Time

Making Plans

When the time was ripe for it in my life as a pastor, and when as an individual I sensed the real need for a time of both rest and study, I went ahead and made plans to take a sabbatical. Post-Vatican II priests have so many pastoral concerns. The workload for us is truly immense. Yet we do what we must, even though with a continually expanding Catholic population, our clergy numbers are considerably less than in times past. A sabbatical helps us regain our spiritual, mental, and intellectual composure so that we might continue on in the work of our call. At the time when I was looking for a place to go, I remembered that Angie had already invited me to stay at their house in Pryor on the reservation. Across the reservation at Crow Agency was the tribe's Little Big Horn College where I could take the classes that I needed. I gave the idea of going to "Crow Country" a lot of thought.

The Journey Continues

Somehow everything fell into place for me to do this. I was even able to get a priest to take my place in my parish while I was gone. And so, on January 3 of 1990, I packed some of my belongings, including a microwave oven and an electric typewriter (for as yet I had not learned any computer skills), and put them into an old Ford truck that I had borrowed from parishioners, and headed for Montana. A visiting Crow, Darrel Nomee, wanted to come along for the ride.

An Eagle

Things went well on the trip. But some pleasant surprises were to await us on the journey. Somewhere on a lonely stretch of road in Nevada near Utah I noticed something dark standing out against the snowy fields at some distance in front of us. It seemed to be some kind of large bird hanging upside down from a power pole line. I sensed that it was an eagle and I was right. Upon closer inspection I became overjoyed for I recognized it as a positive sign that all would go well. I knew that it was a gift for us to ritually utilize in sacred ways. Since it was suspended upside down on the line by only one talon, it looked as if it would be easy to get. But it was quite a bit out of our reach. "What should we do now?" I thought. That was when the skills of my former life as a house painter with my Dad came into play for us.

Though it was late afternoon and we did not have much time to do our work, I checked our map and then headed for the nearest town, Delta, Utah, in order to seek out a hardware store. I thought that an aluminum extension pole would be what we needed, but the store did not have one. I looked around and spotted some wooden poles. I bought several, along with some duct tape, and we raced back to the site. Upon our arrival in that snowy place the sun was just going down. So without delay we put ourselves to work before darkness would soon be upon us.

Darrel jumped up on top of my packed goods on the truck. I handed him the taped-together poles for him to knock the noble raptor off the power line, and on his fourth try the eagle fell into my arms. I let out a joyful sound. By ceremonially burning some sage we gave thanks. Then, after having carefully secured the eagle on the truck, we rejoiced all the way to Logan, Utah. Some time later the feathers were distributed for ceremonial use. What a gift from Creator at the beginning of my sabbatical, I thought. This *journey* was indeed giving life to *the dream.*

Activities

I arrived in the community of Pryor, on the Crow Reservation on a cold January evening. The snow had "drifted" and was blocking both driveway and entrance of the house that I was to live in during my sabbatical time. I had been instructed by Angeline Whiteman to go to the back shed and bring out the sled in order to more easily move the items from my overloaded truck. I looked at the full moon, offered a prayer, and wondered exactly what I was getting myself into. But it was a wonderful beginning for me, a time that was to renew me in my spirit as well as in my mind and in my body. But first I needed to turn the heater on!

Though I helped out occasionally at the local church, I was really there to relax, study, and enjoy life so that I might return to the parish refreshed. Father Randolph Grayck, (O.F.M.Cap.) is a Capuchin Franciscan who speaks the *Apsaalooka* (Crow) language as well as anyone should. He is kind and thoughtful and knows the culture really well after having lived on the reservation for many years. He was especially helpful to me whenever I had a particular question about Crow spirituality or culture. Along with his Capuchin colleagues at Crow Agency and the Lodge Grass area, he makes sure that the People here are well attended to, spiritually speaking.

I spent a lot of my time getting to know everyone around the area, both Indian and non-Indian. At least twice a week I entered the sweatlodge with my soon-to-adopt-me dad Irvin Stuart or his son-in-law Frank Merchant, married to Lou, or my adopted brother Sonny. Actually, Frank is a *Pikuni* (a section of the Blackfeet Tribal confederacy). He would always have a story or two to share about his own tribe's life in the Rocky Mountains section of Montana. I had a lot of fun times with Rocky Bulltail r.i.p., John Plainfeather r.i.p., and Turk Plainbull and their families. Nearby or across the reservation about fifty miles away were my other relatives and friends, members of my future Crow clans: the Greasy Mouths and the Big Lodge folks.

At his special request one cold winter night as we were driving back from Billings to the reservation, Sonny Carlson, a Cheyenne living nearby, informed me that he and I would later on in the springtime fast together in the mountains for four days in a traditional Cheyenne vision quest. His words were both a suggestion and an order for something that he knew needed to happen for both of us as future "brother friends." And so we did. During such times you can really get to know someone else more personally and this

Louella Merchant, my adopted Crow sister

Crow dancer, Crow Agency, Montana

Crow Fair, Montana

always bodes well for the future. Since those sacred four days I have been able to share the experience many times by helping individuals prepare for their own vision quests, their own special times with Creator's creation.

I took classes relating to Crow tribal art, song, and dance at Little Big Horn College. I only wish that I had signed up for Crow language classes as well. Perhaps there will be another time. Anyway, most of the classes were taught bilingually in English and Crow. The teachers really knew their material and wanted to share the knowledge. Every class seemed to have a spiritual dimension to it.

Though some learning took place in the classroom, most of my new Crow knowledge came from individuals who shared both history and ceremonies with me. Among those exceptional individuals who made it a point to reach out to me is Bert Plainbull. His family took me in and always made me feel at home. I remember playing some kind of ball game with everyone one Easter Sunday right after the dinner. Someone called out to me, "Hey, Dances with Crows!" He was jokingly referring to another more well-known White guy, Kevin Costner, who starred in the movie *Dances with Wolves* that had just recently come out. I took it as a compliment! At their house there were always lots of kids running around, plenty of food, and great conversation.

Bert, upon proper spiritual consultation, decided to pass on to me both the right to "pour the water," that is, to lead a Crow sweatlodge ceremony, as well as to build the structure itself. I feel privileged to have received this sacred trust. He wanted me to be able to share the Crow way with people out in California and "to do it the right way." Of course, beforehand I had to provide him with the traditional four special gifts to show that I appreciated what I was receiving. I did so after a period of time. When he was free to pass on the gift of the sweatlodge, we went out in my truck to collect dry cottonwood branches for the fire. He then taught me specifically how to make the fire and to do the ritual correctly. Over the years and along with countless others, I have witnessed many little miracles and answers to prayer in the sweatlodge since that remarkable day. *Ahóo*, Bert, *Itchik* (Thank you, Bert, it's good!).

Sundance Preparations

I recall being invited to observe an "opening of the sacred bundle" ceremony held in Prior one Spring evening. For many of the plains tribes, whose ancestors moved about in prairie places where the buffalo had roamed from ancient times, sacred bundles are still an important part of their spirituality. Essentially, personal medicines, that is, "sacred objects" like eagle or hawk feathers, talons, unique stones, beads, etc. came to be wrapped up in many pieces of soft leather or colored cloth, placed in a specially prepared bag, and kept in a safe place by the one who "owned" the bundle, only to be brought out at ceremonial times, then ritually unwrapped and so displayed that their inherent power might be shared with others, especially in times of healing or for strengthening either individuals or the local band.

On that memorable evening many Sundance songs were heard in the place where we had gathered. Upon arrival I noticed that three Crow medicine men and the local priest, Father Randolph, were seated cross-legged in the middle of the floor, each of these spiritual leaders, in unison with the drumbeat, sounding his eagle-bone whistle with every breath. The energy was captivating, and I knew that something very sacred was happening. This was the time of year when the first thunders are heard by everyone, calling upon bears and rattlesnakes and all other animals (and all people) to wake up and live out correctly our own individual aspects of Akbaatadia's (Creator's) handiwork.

At a certain point in the ceremony, each one of us presented two cigarettes to each spiritual leader, whispering our prayer intentions. The cigarettes were then lined up in front of each holy man and all of them were smoked by them to the accompaniment of drumming and singing. We all waited patiently until the last one was smoked. How it was possible for only four people to smoke all of those cigarettes in such a short time, I will never completely understand! It is widely known that for most Native Peoples throughout the Americas there has always existed a strong spiritual connection between tobacco and prayer. Many folks from other cultures may not probably know this or the meaning of it. Tobacco, when ritually used in a variety of ways, usually signifies a kind of cleansing of the area around the one praying as well as the prayers carried to Creator in the rising smoke. Any negative energy must then dispel itself from the place of gathering.

But smoke and pray they did! Each bundle was then slowly opened, one wrapping at a time, revealing invisible sacred energy. In the presence of the opened bundles the four holy men then proceeded to "doctor," that is, pray for healing by gently but firmly brushing with their eagle wing fans those individuals who came forward. I too came forward and I am glad that I did. Later a potluck feast was shared by all. The People usually gather three more times for this ceremony until the actual Sundance takes place in July or August, as they have done for many generations. On this part of my spiritual passage into "Indian Country" I felt truly blessed and encouraged.

I drew closer to the land during this time and came to recognize my place among all the individuals in my life and in my ministry, both those who cared for me and those that I cared for. It was a renewal of my life as well as my priesthood. I had always felt close to God, but this sacred time apart simply amplified this closeness for me and made it more intimate. During this sabbatical I fished, hunted, hiked, studied, prayed, laughed, cried, visited, traveled, questioned, affirmed, relaxed, celebrated, slept soundly and awoke refreshed; I played, drove, rode, danced, sang, powwowed, joked, and feasted regularly and without shame. I thank God, the Diocese of Monterey, and all the people that I met along the way for this wonderful Life opportunity.

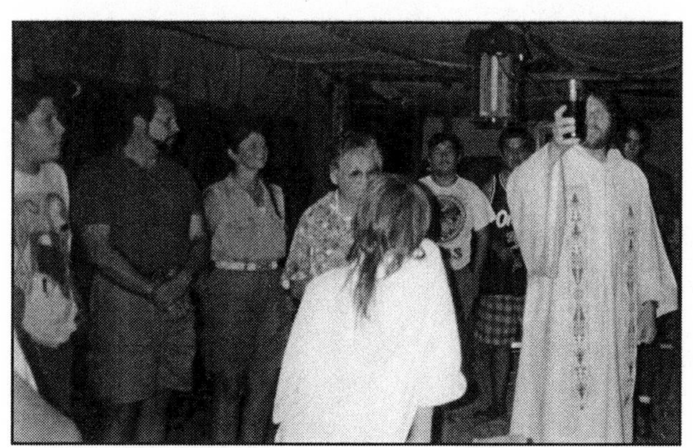

Celebrating a mass with Crow relatives during Crow Fair, Crow Agency, Montana

A Little Bit of Paradise: Second Pastorate: Carmel Valley

In 1993 I became the pastor of Our Lady of Mount Carmel Church in Carmel Valley. It was a paradise for me from the first moment of my arrival. I had served for about ten years in a semi-urban setting, and now there was plenty of space and lots for me to do in a more amplified, country setting. The parishioners were, it seemed, also eager for some kind of positive change, and so I set myself to promote it in the life of the parish.

On the journey of my life, here was a special place where *the dream* was becoming realized from day to day. Both parishioners

Blessing a mountain on the Kirk family's Oak Ridge Ranch, Carmel Valley, California, 1998

and longtime friends could see that I was now experiencing a special kind of intense growth that was happening in my very being as a person. I truly felt it from the inside out and the outside in. Somewhat hard to describe, it seemed to be for me some kind of ongoing personal fulfillment connected to an inner peace telling me that all is well and all will be well in my life as time goes by.

A Carmel Valley wedding

The Village of Carmel Valley sits in the midst of Esselen Tribe traditional territory, directly on a path that leads from Carmel Mission Basilica. Here I was to come across quite a few individuals and families who let me know that they were undeniably Esselen, at least that part of their blood heritage was Esselen. It seems that this tribe has never been great in numbers in regard to its own members in comparison to the larger Navajo or Lakota ethnic groups. They always had a distinct culture and language, much different from their neighbors, the Salinan, Chumash, or Ohlone Peoples. They excelled in basketry and knew well the cycles of the seasons and how to receive the gifts of Mother Earth and give thanks to Creator for them. They were a mountain people who also felt equally close to the rivers and the ocean. They were a great family of families dispersed throughout forest, mountain, river and ocean. Their descendents today, like many other tribal groups, are doing their best to maintain culture and tribal unity in a modern context, and, though it is difficult on many levels, they do what they can.

A Unique Sweatlodge

As soon as I was settled I set about contacting some Esselens. Parishioners told me that some of the prominent family names were Corona, Hitchcock, Manjares, Meadows, Mondragon, and Nason.

Usually it was through serendipitous encounters, as always for me it seems, that I would run into some of these family members. I recall participating in some ceremonies that the Nasons, Tom and his father Fred, held up at their mountain ranch near Tassajara, "Window to the West."

They had built a large traditional semi-subterranean ceremonial lodge and a related similarly designed sweat lodge. I had never actually seen an example of either one before, and therefore I could only marvel at their simple but powerful architecture. Both edifices have entrances on an incline, so there is a real sense of physically entering into the womb of Mother Earth. Their circular roofs are made of wooden beams radiating from a pitched center. As they are covered with earth, the structures blend in well with the natural environment. In the more ample gathering structure four large posts hold up the roof and allow for a central fire pit that throws its shadows against the wall. All around the earthen wall of this sacred place there are seating areas in the adobe and areas behind them to

Esselen sweat lodge ceremony, Pine Valley, near Carmel Valley, California

recline or store items. The sweat lodge is much smaller, similar in shape, and the sacred hot stones are placed within the area of the four posts that also support its roof. Even though they are somewhat recently built, such Native ceremonial architecture speaks to me of ancient mystery. They really come alive when the folks gather in them. Modern time seems not to exist inside, only sacred time connected to the ancestors and Creator.

Once I received an invitation from Tom Nason to participate in a sweat lodge and ceremonial campout in the remote Pine Valley area of the Big Sur Mountains. Those invited were part of the Four Winds Council and the Esselens were hosting this sacred time together. I recall that monks from the Catholic monastery on the Big Sur coast, Buddhist practitioners from the Tassajara area, psychologists, along with some others unknown to me, were present. Genaro Arista, a *temascalero*, a member of our own sweatlodge group, and I represented our parish. We hiked down the mountains from our direction, the east. When at last we reached the meeting place, we noticed that everyone else had travelled somewhat leisurely on horseback. Though quite weary from the journey, by some miracle of timing we ourselves had arrived just in time.

This gathering, representing peoples coming from the directions of the four winds, prayed, ate, and played in harmony. As different world religions seemed to be represented in this sweat lodge ceremony, their unique song resonances and rhythms expressed powerful but prayerful sentiments. This happened to be the first time that I heard Buddhist chants immediately following Christian and Native songs in a sweat lodge ceremony, and it was a bit historic for some of us, I suppose. Afterwards, food and song around the fire continued to bring everyone together on other levels. Since the meal was vegetarian, I was not so thrilled at dinner time, especially after such a hike and intense ceremony. But it was nourishing, I must admit, and healthily good for us.

We spent the night in a teepee that, evidently, had a tear near the top. Not realizing this due to the darkness, we inadvertently put our sleeping bags directly under it. The surprisingly cold night brought us an extra surprise: a long downpour of heavy, cold rain. Needless to say, we had a difficult, soggy sleep that night. At about 4:30

A drum song resounds in Carmel Valley, 2002

Quiché Mayan friend, Tek Itzep Diego Pasá, and Francia Alá

AM, while it was still pitch black outside, Genaro, who needed to be at work in Seaside very early, and I started to ascend the mountain. What a unique experience. Now I realize how some of the early explorers to this land might have felt on day and night forced marches during inclement weather! Everything was wet and so were we. Nevertheless, it was so very wonderful to soon experience the morning sun warming the earth all around us, bathing everything in gentle light. The song of the birds along with their special spatial movements in the sky made the difficult climb both easy and unforgettable. I will always remember that special time in Pine Valley.

Sometimes our reputations precede us. While living in Carmel Valley people would often request "Indian ceremonies" at a "celebration of life" memorial service or even the blessing of a home, a ranch, or animals. Since there are always lots of horses nearby, many folks do make such requests. I am sure that Saint Francis of Assisi, the patron of animals and ecology, would be proud of me, even though the burning sage smudge would most likely not be what he was used to so long ago in those hills of Umbria in Italy. Sometimes my Quiché Mayan friend, Tek Itzep Diego, and Francia Alá would help. At other times, sometimes at a parish mass, I would utilize, or spiritually activate, eagle feathers in some special blessing, as long as everyone present understood and respected this sacred action. The assembly always appreciated these kinds of borrowed cultural rites, it seemed to me, even though at one time they were celebrated uniquely and quite naturally by the People themselves.

Powwows in Prison

A couple of times powwows were held at Soledad Prison, about forty miles away from my home. On these occasions I helped nearby Indian communities to organize them. Such cultural activities like these had never been held before in that prison. Realizing that the inmates had no access to important items like feathers of any kind, I brought along a good number of fine looking plumes for the inmates to use or wear during our time together with them. Of course, all the feathers needed to be returned at the end of the evening. Once the powwow got going and prayer was offered, the drums and voices began to sound out. At first the fellows were shy to dance in the circle. They just sat and watched us. But then, when we called them into the action, a few at a time lost their shyness and they had no more difficulty. The dance circle then grew quite large. Only children and young people were missing. But that was understandable, given the environment.

A special prayer from Bishop Ryan was prayed in front of the inmates towards the close of the day's activities and then, with an inmate and his visiting mother, I headed up an eagle feather blessing ritual for everyone gathered in the sacred circle, during which the singers slowly and respectfully hit the drum. A few drops of water and some red earth were poured on the palm of each one's hand, after which I blessed the individual inmate on the head with the eagle feathers that I was carrying. I believe that it was an effective healing ceremony for everyone concerned.

Later we feasted on traditional foods like salmon, venison, buffalo, and the like that someone had thoughtfully donated. The post dinner activity consisted of a "give-away ceremony." That is, the inmates gave to each of the visitors some handcrafts that they had made in advance. Items like drawings and beadwork came home with us on that day. The warden is to be commended for allowing such joy to move among at least a few of those who are incarcerated in such a difficult environment. I only wish that this type of activity was a regular event on the prison calendar. Powwows are not only enjoyable events for all those who are present, but they are also spiritual activities filled with prayers to Creator that are activated by the drum and people dancing, their feet and bodies moving about in a sacred circle that represents all life.

Prior to these powwows, I would receive requests for our own Kateri Circle to send down lava rocks and sage for the Native inmates' own sweat lodge ceremonies. Such things were always difficult to get inside the prison. The Catholic chaplain, Father Joel Almendras, was always helpful and understanding of their needs. Even the sacred pipe of the inmates, the *cannupa*, was kept in his office for safekeeping.

Priests Serving California Native People

A few of us priests in California worked with native communities. Usually they would serve the Hupa, Yurok, or Karuk Peoples in the northern part of the state, or the Ipai, Tipai or Kumeyaay Peoples near the Mexican border. I, however, have always served in a regular multicultural parish assignment that usually had some Native constituency, though perhaps small and difficult to measure. But it was always challenging and good for me.

One time, after having come to know a few of these priests who served Native Peoples in our state of California, we decided to band together to share our experiences, wisdom, and resources on behalf of those we were serving. On one occasion we invited Bishop Ryan to our meeting, praying with him in the Indian way. He became our representative to the California Bishop's Conference in Sacramento. We planned for many things to happen in our various pastoral situations, but, alas, several of these priests became transferred too soon to other assignments and we were never really able to realize most of our plans.

I remember that at one of these meetings we talked about rendering a new image of Blessed Kateri and composing a special prayer to encourage ministry vocations among young Native people. I asked a well-known artist from Soquel, Patricia Kay Shubeck, my special "godsister," to prepare a more "Native-looking" line drawing image of this saint to accompany a prayer that I had written. It seems that this work might become properly promoted in the near future. We also thought about organizing an annual time of fasting with

Native People throughout California, perhaps in the springtime or coinciding with Lent, each person according to her or his own tribal tradition, and respectfully coordinated with a local spiritual leader. Perhaps events like this might help unite tribes and bands in a much more profound way, as well as help them to explore or even restore some other aspects of their own distinct cultural and spiritual heritages. Only positive spiritual power and energy to be shared with others to do only good will come from such activities, I believe.

American Indian Movement Personalities

My good friend, Paul Peralta, has many Indian friends, some quite famous, a few of which were founding members of the American Indian Movement (A.I.M.). Over the years he and his wife, Karen, have taken the time to be most supportive of my personal and pastoral efforts. Once, Paul and I had a surprise opportunity to visit that controversial country of Cuba, a few years before the changeover of leadership from Fidel Castro to his brother Raúl. Our original plan was to visit some of the Mayan temples in the Yucatan Peninsula of Mexico, but once in Cancún, another friend of his convinced us to take the short 50-minute flight to Havana.

My friend, Paul Peralta, and I at a powwow, Hollister, 1989

Ox team ploughing sugar cane fields near Cienfuegos, Cuba, 2001

A fine Brazilian soccer player, Filip, with Leon Stiffarm, after Sundance Ceremony, near Sandy, Oregon, 2001

Crow Sundance center pole, 1993

We found the people to be most hospitable and gracious to us in every way. Contemporary Cuba displays both its colonial past as well as its architecture and automobile remnants dating from the 40s and 50s eras, just prior to the revolution. The revolution seems to be continuing, but in some kind of adapted form. Perhaps the time is very near for Cuba to experience some kind of "normalized" relationship with the USA, and, it is hoped, with a final end to the suffering caused by the embargo imposed on this island country of such wonderful people. No matter what form its own government will maintain or transform for the future, I pray daily for positive change for these people, however it will be. I am much encouraged by letters from folks we met, each one inquiring about my next visit. I want to praise all the Cuban people who were so hospitable to me during my brief stay on their island.

Though there had been several waves of occupation over the millennia, the least ancient inhabitants of this island (Caobana) are called Tainos, the same name one encounters in describing inhabitants of nearby islands like Hispaniola (Quisqueya), which nowadays is divided into Haiti and the Dominican Republic, and also Puerto Rico (Boriken). Though the stay in Cuba was relatively short for us, it was really quite bountiful for me because I was able to find some traces of its more ancient Taino heritage, like a replica ceramic bowl and ceremonial stone axe-head, as well as some rare books on its indigenous presence, and bring them home with me. For those who know how to see, there are many signs of living "Taino-ness" in the Cuba of today. I understand that the ancient bloodline in the eastern section of the island is strong and that, like Tainos of other islands, they are in the midst of a cultural resurgence.

Oh, I might add that on my way back from the town of Cienfuegos to Havana to concelebrate the Sunday morning liturgy with the cardinal, I got both a flat tire and a speeding ticket! Needless to say, I was too late for the mass. And that is not all. As chance would have it, and not through my own fault this time, my return flight to Mexico took off without me, leaving me to survive with only my last $38.00 cash in my wallet (one did not use U.S. credit cards at that time in Cuba). I prayed that there would be no international incident connected to my presence in such an embargoed nation, as well as my safe return home. I must admit that I was a bit uneasy at that moment until the next day when I actually sat down on the plane headed back to Mexico. But that is another story…!

As I mentioned, Paul happens to count among his friends well-known, and one might say, for some people controversial, individuals like: Dennis Banks (Anishnabe), Floyd Westerman r.i.p. (Lakota), Janet McCloud r.i.p. (Tulalip), as well as Mary Jane Wilson (Anishnabe). During a surprise visit to her home in Washington, he and I enjoyed Janet's wonderful hospitality and were treated to a sumptuous feast of cracked crab. Another time, Mary Jane surprised me one evening by using my place for a special Bear Medicine healing ceremony. Her healing abilities were manifested before our very eyes in a ritual that took place in the semi-darkness right by the fireplace. The patient became much improved as a result of her traditional medicinal skills. Another time I witnessed Dennis Banks giving Paul the name "Tobacco Dancer" during his adoption ceremony. Throughout various moments over the last few years I have been privileged to experience some brief encounters with Floyd Westerman, a famous Lakota film star and activist for Native rights. He is probably most well-known for his role in the ever popular movie, *Dances with Wolves.*

Grow Ventre Sundance

Leon Stiffarm, a Montana Gros Ventre tribal member who now lives near Portland, Oregon, once paid me a surprise visit along with his wife. We spent some time visiting my "museum" of native items. After we got to know each other for a while, he asked me for a four-year commitment to help him with a traditional Sundance that he planned to hold later on a mountain ranch. I was taken aback. What a privilege. Over the years, most Sundances have been closed to outsiders due to many cultural and religious misunderstandings on the part of outsiders. Leon is a man who, like some others of our time, is ready and willing to share his ancient spiritual heritage with non-Native people. He does so with knowledge, respect, patience, and openness to each person who comes to him. He is at the same time strict and somewhat disciplinary with the fasting dancers, but his gentleness also carries them through their four-day ordeal. Though the Sundance experience is intense, I have seen the great changes that come over those who listen to him and follow his wisdom in this sacred ceremony. Blessing upon blessing continues to flow forth to the People. As I fulfilled my commitment to the Sundance, I too experienced some blessings as a result of this special prayer. May Leon continue to be led by the Spirit of God!

My Book on Native Spirituality: *People of the Circle, People of the Four Directions*

I have been told that I have amassed an outstanding library of books and audiovisuals that pertain to Native Peoples of this hemisphere and that many articles included in my private museum perhaps are among some of the best in private collections on the West coast. At first I just collected Indian books for personal enjoyment and study, but as the years gradually passed I began to receive requests to use my resources to help students and other individuals, both Native and non-Native, in their own pursuit of knowledge. Other than the books, the art works and ceremonial items are mostly gifts received from my ever-growing list of friends in faraway places. It gives me great pleasure to loan a book out or explain the origin and use of an artifact to an interested inquirer. This invariably gives me an opportunity to launch into a story about the people connected to the item in their hands.

All things considered, and thanks to the freedom and wonderful encouragement given to me by the parishioners and friends of Our Lady of Mount Carmel Church, I was able to dedicate some time to prepare and complete *People of the Circle, People of the Four Directions.* I drew from my own library and others as well in order to facilitate my choices of important quotations that are included in my work. I know that among many folks the book has found favor as a helpful resource for the numerous cultures and spiritualities of the First Peoples of "Turtle Island," as it is endearingly called by some tribes.

As the manuscript was almost ready to go to press, I happened to be invited to a buffalo steak dinner at a local restaurant in Carmel Valley by my good friend Sharman Haverly. Between bites of food, she asked me if I had gotten all the photos ready to illustrate the

José Ortíz, wearing Taino headdress

book's text. I said, "Yes, except that I do not really have the Caribbean area properly represented." As chance would have it, or, as Creator would have it, she then proceeded to tell me that in her purse she had some phone numbers of people in Puerto Rico that I should definitely contact about the needed photos. She and a well-known Shoshone medicine man, Corbin Harney, had just a few years before gone to the *Isla del Encanto* (the Enchanted Island) at the invitation of some Tainos and had done ceremonies and built sweatlodges for prayer. They had, as I was to come to realize, helped to further the activation of some of the modern Taino tribal resurgence. "Wow! I'll get on it!" I exclaimed.

As soon as possible I met with my good Puerto Rican friend and parishioner, José Ortíz, a professor of Spanish language at the Defense Language Institute in Monterey. We called some of the telephone numbers and very soon reached Doctor Ramón Nenadich, a social sciences professor at the University of Puerto Rico at Rio Piedras, San Juan. He promised to send some photos of recent Taino events and, much to our surprise, invited us to become delegates to the first Native Gathering of the Americas to be held in Puerto Rico. We accepted. Not knowing what to expect, inside myself I sensed that something important was brewing. I will tell more of this later. *The journey and the dream* were becoming more manifest, I felt.

Some years back, while on my sabbatical with the Crows, my first book, *Celebrating the Earth,* had come out in publication. Angie and Norman Whiteman had helped me to feast its arrival with a pizza meal the day that I received my first copy hot off the press. It was a really happy time of life for me, and especially to be "published." Shortly after this it was suggested by a number of friends and some other interested persons that I write something more specifically concerning Native Peoples, as it was common knowledge that many books of the time often contained incorrect statements, offered prejudicial points of view, or promoted a revisionist sense of history which only favored the newcomers to these ancient lands.

I thought about this for some time and considered doing something relating to the various tribal Sundances as they have been ritually led in the past and are celebrated in our present time by peoples of the plains areas. I did indeed take up some specific studies of these unique ceremonies, but did not feel ready to pursue the particular proposal very far. As I was a priest, and not a trained anthropologist or ethnologist, I questioned whether I would be credible enough to those outside my usual spheres of activity. But, little by little, the encouragement of others made me act on my basic intuitions, even though I found myself wandering away from the original topic of research. "What should I really write about," I thought.

For many years I had considered how tribe after tribe related to the four directions according to their own particular cosmologies. I also knew that the all-inclusive circle had been important as well as a centering symbol for eons unknown. Doing special activities in relation to the sacred number 4 had been a practice of the People throughout these lands from time immemorial as well as now. While living in Carmel Valley, I felt that the time was right for me to begin to write such a book about these concepts in order to help both the general reader interested in things indigenous as well as First Nations folks. And indeed it seems to have been gone well. I even felt "inspired" to go ahead with the project, especially as things kept falling into place regarding it. After a couple of years of intense busyness, and with a full schedule of active parish work, *People of the Circle, People of the Four Directions* entered the world of published books in 1999.

A Pomo Medicine Woman

Years ago a wonderful woman came into my life and her name was Bernice Torres, a member of the Pomo Tribe of Northern California. It must have been around 1977 when I was introduced to her originally by Mary Riotutar, my Chippewa-Cree friend, at a powwow in Aptos. As the social introductions were taking place, we heard the intertribal dance call from the emcee and I invited her to step up with me into the dance circle. Much older than I, she mentioned that she had never danced with a priest before. I replied with something like, "Be careful, you might be dancing with a devil!" and she laughed, looking at me intently. I did not know at the time that she was a well-renowned medicine woman and came from a long line of healers in her tribe.

A few years later she paid me a surprise visit at my Castroville parish. With nothing particular in mind, she just wanted to chat over a cup of coffee, and so we did just that. Meanwhile in the background we could hear the usual busy activity noises of the church office and the phone ringing constantly. All of a sudden she asked if she could sing me an Indian song. Surprised, I said yes to her request. She stared into my eyes and sang something in her own language. It was nice to listen to for it had a very gentle melody. When I asked what it meant, she laughingly and in a child-like way said that she was singing about my beard and handsome face. I am sure I blushed deeply at that moment, feeling both amazement and privileged at the same time. All I could do was thank her. We finished our coffee and soon, smiling like a happy child, she returned to her car. I was left with such a good feeling inside.

A couple of years later, upon hearing that she was starring in a made-for-TV movie called *Grand Avenue,* I became curious to see it. It was well worth seeing, for it showed the difficulties of raising Native children in a multicultural neighborhood where violence often occurs. Another time, on a Saturday of Holy Week, the day before Easter, she once again surprised me with another brief and unexpected visit, this time at my church in Carmel Valley. A group of us were decorating the church and she was on her way to an Esselen tribe celebration nearby in the mountains by Tassajara. Before she left, I invited her to come back the next day to sing a Pomo song at the Mass. "What kind?" she inquired. "Oh, something about new life," I said. Her smile indicated that she would be back the next morning. As she stood in front of the altar and shook her butterfly cocoon rattle, her voluminous voice filled the church. The assembly of worshippers was both silent and happily astounded. Nobody had ever heard something like this at church before, but they liked it. The applause was spontaneous and lengthy.

Shortly after this I was asked to appear at a special gathering being given in her honor in Monterey. I walked in somewhat late, trying to be discreet about my entrance, but she saw me and called me up in front of everyone. She then spoke to everyone about how I had helped her spiritually in her life. I was not really aware that I had done very much, but she continued on, heaping praises upon me. I slinked away, slightly embarrassed, but deep down inside myself I felt very pleased with her affirmation of my work with the local Native community. Lamentably, not long after this I got news that she had passed on. A memorial tile honorably placed in the Steinbeck Center in Salinas, California, helps to remind us yet of her influential goodness.

Bear Dances

Many tribes have dances and songs to honor the bear. Some are far from their original homelands where there are no extant bears, but they continue to do the dances nonetheless. It is important for them to continue this tradition because it connects them through dance, song, and drumbeat to their places of origin and helps maintain their spirituality. The California tribes also have their bear dances, some lasting many days. The preparation for these dances is extensive and is considered an honor and a blessing for all who participate. They are not usually advertised to the general public lest they be considered a show or entertainment of some kind. Some tribes who had lost some of their dance and song traditions are in the rescue mode for their culture and, happily, are gradually being gifted with some of these dances and sacred songs by neighboring tribes who have never really lost them. And so the bear dances continue on from time immemorial to the present generation.

One unique aspect of the bear dances that I have witnessed during the late evening ceremonies of the annual Honoring of the Elders Powwow held in the mountains above Watsonville is the way that the bear dancers enter the sacred circle. First, all is silent and dark except for the large fire in the center of the dance circle. After appropriate prayer offerings of fish, berries, and honey are placed in the fire to spiritually attract the bears and a special song is sung, grunting sounds coming from the direction of the forest are heard by everyone present. Then, one by one the bears enter, each one attended to by an assistant who continuously wafts smoke from large wands of sage or mugwort over them. A song accompanies the bears as they circle around, grunting all the time. Then, all of a sudden, something happens that is difficult to explain. In some mystical way, it seems that bears appear to be really present, much more than the personas of the actual dancers themselves. In the last dance each bear places a paw on the left shoulder of the one just ahead and the dancing continues. Shortly after this, everyone is invited to enter the circle to dance with the bears, making the same formation while following the same steps. Round and round everyone goes, and faster and faster until there is a sudden stop. People then return to their places as the bears, still grunting, slowly dance out of the circle into the forest. This is a springtime renewal ceremony, a sacred time when no one needs to be afraid of the bear. Only blessings are sought from Creator by means of the spirit of the bear.

In May of 2001 a young bear was noticed in a tree in downtown Carmel. One hundred fifty years ago, this would probably not be such a surprising discovery. Very few people even remotely consider that bears exist nearby this popular tourist town. Yet they do survive, though small in number, in isolated sections of the Los Padres National Forest further south near the Big Sur area. Sadly, this lone bear cub that had sought refuge in a tree, was shot with a tranquilizing gun, and simply fell out of the tree and accidentally was killed. Everyone was sad and shocked at what had occurred. Its death was not intended. The authorities only wanted to tranquilize the little one so as to bring it to a better place out of harm's way. Perhaps, the dosage was too powerful. As the bear fell in the sight of many onlookers, it was instantly killed by the fall.

People, both Native and not, took sides on the issues of what should have been done and what should then be done with the remains of the dead bear. Even some local Native folks were at odds with each other as to which tribal group had the right to respectfully dispose of the carcass after it had been autopsied by the Fish and Game Department. At the time I was privately consulted by one group as to what should be done, so I devised a short "native style" ceremony for the interment of the remains. Things were taken care of by means of prayer, singing and drumming, and all was done respectfully in a secret place in the mountains so that future controversy would be minimal. I felt sad with what had happened, yet pleased that it had become resolved. However, I could not help but think of the times when, at the death of a relative, people often fight with each other as to who should plan the services and exactly how they should proceed and just what they will get from the deceased's estate after the funeral. Perhaps the lowly animals have much to teach us in this regard.

A Four Directions Ceremony and a Lake Circling Blessing

Upon occasion I am asked to share some of my indigenous knowledge with my fellow priests. One day we priests of the diocese all gathered with the bishop in the courtyard of Carmel Mission for a special ceremony. Some local Indian friends were stationed at the points of the cardinal directions, dressed appropriately in traditional regalia, ready to sing with drum, clapper stick, or rattle in hand. Sage, cedar, tobacco, copal, each one coming from the world of sacred plants, burned copiously, their fragrances filling the courtyard. At each direction of east, south, west, and north an appropriate verse from Marty Haugen's "Directional Song" was prayed. The

Intertribal leaders for the Priests' Four Directions Ceremony, Carmel, California, 2000

space was large enough for all us priests to gather in a group and move around the circle, stopping at each direction for a while as a song was sung and prayers were offered. It was a beautiful day and birds and flowers were everywhere. It was also an historic event, as I do not think that such a large quantity of priests had ever gathered on the mission grounds to pray in the Native way in my diocese. It seemed to reverse the ancient Spanish missionary procedure in earlier times of asking the Natives to pray only in the more European church mode.

Another time we were all gathered for a four-day period of spiritual renewal with our bishop at Saint Francis Retreat, San Juan Bautista. A visiting bishop was also present with us. I had devised a service of Morning Prayer whereby we all followed the circle around the small lake situated on the property, stopping four times along the way at the cardinal directions to pray for the people of our parishes. The drum echoed across the water and everyone sounded their rattles or little bells in unison at the appropriate times. I remember that the visiting bishop was quite animated with the whole affair and he really enjoyed making lots of smoke with the sage wand held in his hand. It was a sight to behold. Even the hawks looking on from the trees seemed to enjoy themselves with us. As I looked into the faces of all the participants I know that they were simultaneously experiencing joy, relief from stress, some humor, as well as a crash-course in Native Spirituality 101. People still remember that day and at times remind me of it. I believe that in some way or other the power of these ceremonies positively influenced each one present, while at the same time educating us in the ways of Native People. It was a happy time for us, but it served also as an object lesson on what we can share with our parishioners if we only take the time.

An Historic Funeral

Frances Subia (Subilla) Chioino Adams, a Chumash elder and matriarch for a large extended family, baptized at Mission San Luis Obispo in the year 1919, was mourned at a vigil and funeral mass in Seaside's Saint Francis Xavier Church many years later in 2000. Native ceremonies were commingled with Catholic ritual and everyone had an opportunity to participate in some meaningful way. The sounds of the clapper stick, the rattle, and the drum made this special farewell so significant. One elderly couple even danced out of the church at the closing song. Such a sacred event, sad though it was, was able to bring together a diverse community of Native and non-Native folks because the ceremonies were celebrated intertribally in the context of a richly expressive and meaningful liturgy. It also was a kind of "living proof" that, though on the surface they might seem contradictory, differing spiritualities are indeed able to cross and make sense to those folks carrying within their beings one, two, or more spiritualities, either personal or inherited. I have seen this happen over and over again in my experience. Though their ambiance is urban, this particular part of the well-known Chiono family-clan continues to pass on their Indian ways to the newer generation.

A School Presentation

It has always been my custom to respond immediately to requests to visit schools to speak to students of all ages about my own experiences with Native Americans. Usually I would bring with me musical instruments, artifacts, headdresses and the like so that everyone could listen and feel something that might broaden their understanding. One time I was invited to go to York School, a private high school under the auspices of the Episcopal Church. Not realizing beforehand that I was to address the entire assembled student body along with all their teachers and counselors, I quickly discovered that to make this happen properly I must call upon my most trusted and worthy friend, Allison Gardner who proudly claims her Arapaho heritage, to help me.

I began by asking the students if they had any Native blood. I was taken by surprise as a young man from the Dominican Republic immediately announced that he was Taino. Others came forward with the truth of their own tribal background. These became my helpers as I handed each one an instrument or a headdress. Pretty soon I had a lot of people who were ready for something to happen. I taught them a song and everyone moved from side to side in a simple dance step. Without much coaxing, the energy and movement at that moment was incredible. Everything and everyone gathered became alive and part of what was going on, irrespective of their claiming to be "part Indian" or not. There was lots of laughter interspersed with many wonderful questions from the youth that the presentation went overtime, so caught up was everyone in the activities and having such a good time.

Blessing of Monterey Bay

I have always been interested in ecology and our human role in maintaining good balance by what we do while we live on and with this fragile planet called Earth. Indeed my first book, *Celebrating the Earth,* attempted to share some of my ideas about ecological practices from the aspect of ancient, modern, and creative worship practices. In 2000 the local rabbi, Bruce Greenbaum and I, along with a few more local ministers, took some time to offer prayers for the Carmel River and its environs in order to draw attention to the importance of water in our community. Then in 2002, led by Reverend Deborah Streeter, a number of us local spiritual leaders gave thanks for and blessed the waters of Monterey Bay's National Marine Sanctuary. Including some local tribal representatives, Buddhist, Christian, Jewish, and Moslem spiritual leaders each took part in the ceremony.

Celebrating an ecumenical/inter-religious Blessing of Monterey Bay (organized by Rev. Deborah Streeter, at my left) Monterey, California, 2004

Children also had their role to play. It was beautiful that day and everyone felt that the prayers coming from all the right sources, our sincere human hearts, would be well received and become beneficial in uncountable ways both for the present and future generations that would come to live in our region.

Native Gathering of the Americas

But to get back to the significance of those important phone calls to Puerto Rico encouraged by Sharman Haverly, I would have to say that the *Primer Encuentro Indígena de las Américas* (the First Native Gathering of the Americas), to which I was thrilled to also have been invited, was to become something that really opened up my eyes to glimpse the larger, more international, world of Native Peoples. Twelve other gatherings have followed the first, many of them held in different countries. Some delegates turn out to be usual participants, while others arrive new each year. It is an event that draws many people together to celebrate their "Indian-ness," their "Indigenous-ness," through ceremonies, discussions of common problems, food, and friendships. In relation to the dominant societies in which they live, they see themselves as a sign of a better way to relate to, to protect, and to be good stewards of, our island home, commonly known as Mother Earth. Subsequent editions of my book allowed me to include portraits of some of these delegates as well as photos showing ceremonial activities. I felt that such images would amplify the reader's understanding of the text and give it a more contemporary feel. "We are still here" is a refrain that I have heard over and over in their different languages. It attests that the Native past is very much alive in the present. By means of my book I wanted to add to that testimony.

I arrived in San Juan, Puerto Rico, in March of 1998. Luggage and all and not knowing exactly where I was going to in this strange yet beautiful land, I eventually made it to the Gathering's opening ceremony in the *Jardín Botánico*, the well known tropical botanical garden that is visited daily by individuals and families who like to stroll about, becoming more familiar with native plants of the island. One open area was filled with what seemed to be about one thousand or more people. Some, the delegates and special participants were ethnically clothed, while others were more representative of the contemporary island populace. I was warmly welcomed, my luggage being placed in a safe place, food was offered me, and then I was invited to say something to the crowd. Nervous as I was, still feeling jet lag, and realizing that I had to address everyone in Spanish, I said something to them about myself and my relationship to Native Peoples, thanking them all for the invitation and opportunity to share with them; it was something about me being with them to learn and also that I experienced myself as a kind of person who networked to bring diverse people together, especially native People from up and down the Americas. Was I relieved when, despite my broken Spanish, they cheered and applauded! It was a good beginning, I thought, and I wondered what else might be in store.

The dances of the Taino People are wonderful; they seem to exhibit a direct relation to many other sacred spatial movements that I have seen in the Amazon, especially those that call for the formation of lines of women and men and a special rhythmic stamping of the left feet in unison as they move about in circles or spirals. Their past tells of an ancient migration from the mainland of South America (modern Colombia, Venezuela, Guyana, Surinam, French Guiana, and Brazil) to the Caribbean islands. Their pre-Columbian life might seem most idyllic to many of us nowadays. But then there came to their shores "permanent visitors" from across the sea. As a result of this first contact over five hundred years ago, on many levels Tainos (and their neighboring Caribs) have experienced an enduring pain. History tells us of similar stories in other parts of the Western Hemisphere. Yet Tainos continue to exist, especially in the diaspora in places like New York, New Jersey, Connecticut, Florida, and Los Angeles, despite what had until recently been taught in the history books, though perhaps in ways that are not dissimilar to those of the Native People of our mainland. They live within a dominant society and struggle to maintain their unique identity even though some might consider them to be extinct, few in number, or lacking authentic knowledge of their culture. Perhaps it is the same for any one of us. We all experience the tension, healthy or other, between individual and communal values.

It seemed that all of Puerto Rico knew about this gathering. We stayed in the university's dorms, ate at the faculty lounge, gave presentations to the students, shared ceremonies, dances, prayers, and were given lots of opportunities around the island to get to know each other as delegates and to meet other *Boricuas*, Puerto Ricans.

We visited most of this enchanted island and put on an intertribal ceremony at the Caguana Ceremonial Park near Utuado. For me, this sacred place breathed of antiquity and ceremony. It is a very spiritual place and it would behoove every visitor to spend some time there in meditative activity. My fellow delegates were of top order. There were Aztecs, Tzotsils and Mayans from Mexico, shamans from Ecuador and Venezuela, people from *Rapa Nui* (Easter Island), Mapuches from Argentina, Kunas from Panama, a Carib from Dominica and delegates from Chile, Brazil, and Canada. Many represented tribes from the United States. Some were anthropologists, others were known for their expertise in Native history or present concerns with their respective governments. A sense of unity and *comraderie* developed very quickly. I seemed to be the only Catholic priest among the delegates. Though my being an ordained Catholic priest was not as important as the focus of the time together, one by one, different delegates and other islanders mentioned they were glad that I was participating, even though they did not really expect a priest to be among them. Personally, it felt good to also be a minority (a Celt on both sides of my family, an inquisitive non-Native) in the midst of such a diverse intercultural and international majority.

The week's activities included plenty of sharings as well as heated discussions concerning such topics as cultural survival and government, military or international business interferences in Native affairs. One might consider the Zapatista Movement in Mexico, or the destructive armament and war games pollution due to the former presence of the U.S. military on the Puerto Rican island of Vieques, or the genocide practiced on Native Peoples in Central America in more recent times, or perhaps even the planned eventual extinction of the Indians of this country over the last couple of centuries. Often we allow ourselves to promote revisionist history interpretations of past events. Sometimes we are comfortable with promoting good organizations that care for nearly extinct wildlife species, but are

Taino dance, Aguas Buenas, Puerto Rico, 2008

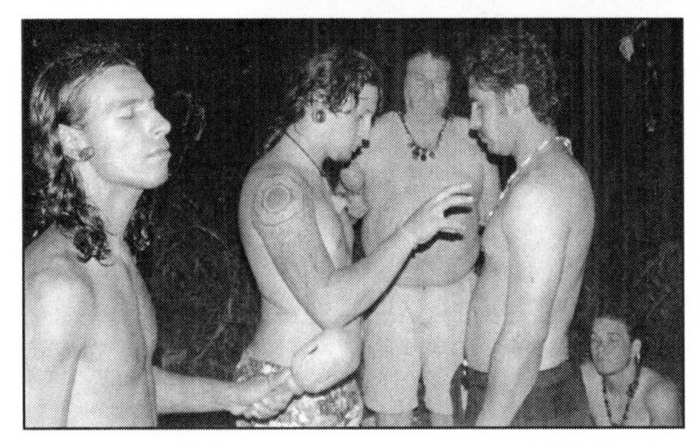

Sharing in Taino healing blessing near Ponce, Puerto Rico, 2008

often not as sensitive about the endangered human cultures that are, through no choice of their own, caught up in the midst of catastrophic modern world changes. There was much to learn from each other and much to discuss as we sought out solutions.

Over the years, since that first eventful gathering when I became introduced to the more "internationally intertribal" reality of the First Nations of the Americas, I have had occasion to make and visit newly-made friends living in very exotic places and also have received into my own home and parish setting some amazingly humble yet dignified individuals. Among many, one such visitor is Ramiro Millán.

With Shaman José Luis Piaroa and Nancy Guzmán after blessing waters of Vieques Island which had been polluted by former military war games armaments, Puerto Rico, 2001

Ramiro

Ramiro Millán

Ramiro is one of those people who mysteriously enter into one's life when least expected. As I remember the occasion, it was one of the last days of the Gathering in Puerto Rico. All of us delegates had attended a musical celebration in the colonial section of Old San Juan. As we were getting ready to leave later that evening, I took a few moments to look up at the full moon and stars that were shining so brightly to give thanks to God for the privilege of being part of this wonderful event. Suddenly someone came up to me dressed, I thought, as if he were a movie star or a model for a clothing magazine. After timidly introducing himself he said that shortly before he had attended a spiritual meeting of some kind and was advised to come to our Gathering that evening where he would meet someone who would help guide him on his spiritual path. He felt that I might be such a person. I was not sure what to say at that moment. We chatted a little, exchanged addresses, and said farewell. A few months later Ramiro and his girlfriend Sofia paid me a visit in Carmel Valley for a few days. During that time we had a lot of opportunities to get to know each other and to further our knowledge of things both spiritual and indigenous. This somewhat "will o' the wisp" friend is always a joy to be around, whenever it happens! Over the years, this one special serendipitous meeting has led to many other wonderful shared memories of new friends meeting other new friends and so on. I look forward to more of this in the future. What a gift friendship is! It has so many spiritual dimensions, each one waiting to be explored as Life's time goes by. As *the journey* continues, friends help catalyze *the dreams* that are inside us.

Gregorio

Gregorio Cortez Cadales is a young member of the Hiwi (Guajibo) tribe from Coromoto Village, near Puerto Ayacucho, Amazon State, Venezuela. At the Gathering he indicated that he would really like to come to California for a visit. Some years later I picked him up at the San Francisco airport, immediately whisking him down to San Juan Bautista Mission for a performance of the Pastorela (a Christmas shepherd's play) performed by Teatro Campesino, a Mexican-American drama company led by the renowned Luis Valdéz, which bilingually and multiculturally celebrates native identity and spiritual tradition. I am sure that jetlag had set in on Gregorio; however he was alert to the performance and very open to meeting lots of new friends. I remember also that he was continually shaking from the cold. A California December for him was not exactly the same as a tropical December in the Amazon! He was to stay for a couple of weeks, but heavier than usual rains in Venezuela did not allow for jets to land safely and so he was forced to remain an extra month with us. By then he was somewhat proficient in English, all things considered. He had a special attachment for my mother who, in her own Scottish way, regularly offered him many cups of tea and little snacks. I know he appreciated all the attention. Present for a book signing party that was held for me, he even autographed a picture of himself that was in my book. At Christmas he was quite amused by a Christmas stocking stuffed with little goodies. It was a tradition vastly different from his tribe's way of celebrating Christmas joy. Prior to our weekly sweatlodge ceremony, Gregorio included us all in one of his own Amazonian tribal *yopo* rituals. All of those present experienced a deep sense of unity through this exotic rite that allows for a deeper appreciation of God through nature. He was a joy for all who met him, especially since any visitors to us coming from deep in the Amazon are few and far between.

Gregorio Cadales Cortez, Hiwi Tribe, Venezuela, autographing his photo in my book, People of the Circle, People of the Four Directions, *1999*

SANTIAGO

I consider Santiago Obispo to be one of my best friends. He regularly comments to other folks that we are like two brothers, one in South America and the other in North America, and that we are destined to travel together, visiting Native communities, and introducing their distinctive tribal realities to the larger world that we both inhabit. Since my first visit to his and wife Nancy's home, situated in one of the urban neighborhoods of the bustling town of Puerto Ayacucho that is located between the Orinoco River and the Amazonian jungle, he has reciprocated several times by visiting my part of California. He seems to possess a panoramic vision of reality, somehow taking in the whole before the particular. This special gift makes it somewhat difficult for the rest of us who would rather concentrate on the particulars of life first and then take in the larger picture. But Santiago is the man that he is and we seem to get along well together whenever we travel or talk about Native affairs. A librarian by profession, he is definitely an international networking person, seeming to know just about everyone or at least able to seek them out. Often he is called upon to speak at international conferences in regard to the ambiance and the situations of fragility and endangerment of the greater Amazon basin that is shared by several countries.

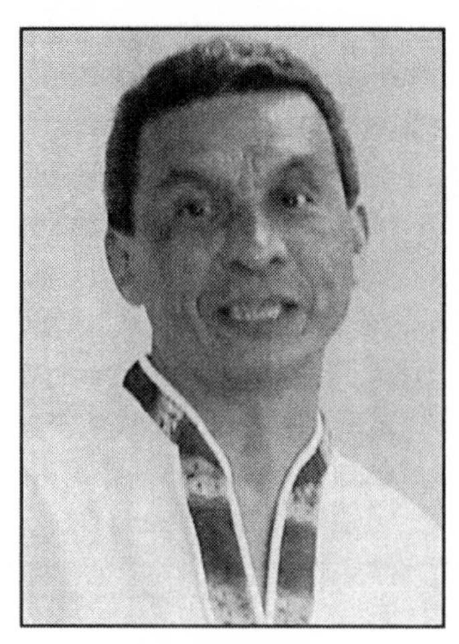

Santiago Obispo

He is especially close to the spiritually powerful shamans José Luis Piaroa and Bolivar. These medicine people and many others like them have no qualms about sharing their "medicines" with outsiders, medicines like *datá, yopo*, tobacco, and *caapi* (*ayahuasca*), as long as the outsiders are respectful. All their medicines are specially made from varieties of leaves, roots, barks and extraordinary, sometimes secret, concoctions made from the internal liquids of plants, most of which may appear quite exotic to most outsiders. Recipes for healing come down from thousands of years of experiential knowledge of how to correctly and safely match up specific pharmacological properties of plants growing in the life-giving rainforest. This ancient and irreplaceable knowledge, accompanied by sacred songs and rituals specific to each tribe, really make healing happen in people's lives. I know the truth of this, for I have shared in many of these healing services at places deep within the jungle. These gentle custodians of the rainforest want to share their ways, but at the same time, they do not want to be "ripped off," thrown to the side, and forgotten by outsiders, be they governments, multinational corporations, pharmaceutical companies, or enterprising individuals.

Though he was raised in the evangelical Christian tradition, and his wife Nancy and the children are Catholic, nevertheless Santiago is really open to many kinds of spiritual practices, especially the traditional ways of the jungle Peoples. Having the ability to talk to anyone at any time about something that seems or later becomes interesting, he is quite able to engage in deep conversation with taxi drivers and waiters and waitresses as well as anyone he finds walking on the street. He makes them all feel important in what they have to share, whatever their educational background or station in life. More than once while at a restaurant or hotel I would feel somewhat embarrassed when he would ask an individual in the lobby or restaurant if she or he were an Evangelical. For me, this is a question that is just too personal and usually does not need to come up in most conversations with persons hardly known. But he seems to get away with it. He does this not to make less of Catholics or people of other faiths. It is just his manner. Able to

Piaroa Shaman Bolivar, a friend from Alta Carinagua, Amazon, Venezuela

speak both Spanish and Portuguese fluently, he is also familiar with the Piaroa native language. Language coaches notwithstanding, I must stress that he happens to have the worst pronunciation of English that I have ever heard! Nevertheless, he is a lovable character and very beneficial for forwarding Indian concerns wherever he goes.

On one of my last visits to Caracas, upon picking me up at the airport, Santiago hurriedly told me that we still had a chance to see what was going on at the *XVI Festival Mundial de la Juventud y los Estudiantes* (Sixteenth World Festival of Youth and Students). I must admit that I had no idea of what he was referring to, but we went anyway. Perhaps it was about young people, like the *jongleurs* of the Middle Ages who traversed Europe seeking more of life's meaning than they had experienced at home or the myriads of international "hippies" of some decades past, each one on a *journey* led by a new *dream*. Since he is also a fellow *aventurero* (adventurer) and has traveled with me far into several South American countries, I trusted him wholeheartedly.

This really exciting week-long event was more than I expected. The whole city was swarming with youthful delegates and all goings on were continually televised, even a youth mock International Court bringing the U.S. president to trial for high crimes. Needless to say, he was found guilty. It was obvious that the theme of this festival had to do with countering war and imperialism. However, for many outsiders it would indeed be considered a radical event because most participants and sympathizers seemed to be *izquierdistas* (leftists) politically. I will say more about some of our past *journeys* and future *dreams* later.

Martin

Martin Muñoz is a very special person. A good listener as well as someone who enjoys sharing interesting aspects of his life at a moment's notice, this treasured longtime friend of mine has been quite influential for me, probably more that he would ever realize. Time and time again he would take note of my ideas or stories about adventures in "Indian country" nearby or in some faraway place

Martin Muñoz sharing a personal story by his home fire, San Juan Bautista, California

and then begin to ask detailed questions, immediately causing me to relive those same experiences so as to explain in more depth. He loves the outdoors, especially water, and could easily spend hours meditating in the warm water of a shallow river (or even a spacious bathtub overflowing with soap bubbles!). He bears true witness to his own spirituality, I believe, and, open-mindedly, always loves to talk about "the things of God."

Carmona Family

Ernie and Roseangel Carmona, along with their extended family who live throughout the Salinas area, have been invaluable friends to me over the many years and have always helped me to further my Native experiences. Living as urban Chicanos, they have never forgotten that their spiritual roots are thrust deep in the soil of Mother Earth and by their following of the ways of Jesus they continue to reach out to many others, especially the less fortunate, through their local parish. They have participated in many retreats, mountain fasts, powwows, Aztec ceremonies, Native liturgies, and Indigenous Gatherings of the Americas. Having a tremendous spirit of overflowing hospitality, they are always ready to host visitors from faraway lands, making sure that they return with an abundance of fond memories. I owe much to this impressively generous family.

Santos

Santos Cortes is a young man who recently in 2007 invited me to celebrate his marriage to his charming wife Gina. We all thought that a wedding day would never arrive for him, but it did! I have known Santos since his college years not too long ago when he first came to a sweatlodge ceremony. His hometown in Soledad, California, he now lives with Gina in San Jose, California. Always interested in the military and high-tech modes of communication, nevertheless throughout his whole life he has also been keenly involved in learning as much as possible about his indigenous culture as well. Having also spent time on the family ranch near Ameca, Jalisco, Mexico, he prides himself on possessing a considerable amount of knowledge about the traditional ways of his people.

At this time, in the midst of a busy life, he feels called to work on a doctorate that treats of his own faith and spirituality, indigenous rituals, and how they fit together. I am pleased to help him with this important activity which, I know, will further his experiences among the People. Earlier on he had sought my advice while working on

Santos Cortes and I on Ustupu Island, Panama, for Native Gathering of the Americas, 2000

a master's thesis that at this time also seems to relate to his newer theme, and I was glad to encourage him in his pursuits. It is always good to share important information critical for the educational development of other folks. Not only does doing this make life a bit more interesting, revealing aspects of life hitherto unknown to the learner, but it enhances continuing growth in the life of the one imparting the knowledge. Here one might consider the invaluable influence of grandparents and friends in the developing lives of children and young people.

Santos continues to possess a spirit of adventure coupled with a firm desire to know more about indigenous people, no matter the tribe or heritage. One year we decided to visit some Mesoamerican pyramids, either Aztec or Maya ones, it did not seem to matter at the time. Having only a few days free to do this, we chose to go to Belize because it seemed to be exotic and replete with both jungles and Mayan ceremonial complexes. We carried a camcorder for filming visits to ancient excavated sites. Along the way we conversed with lots of Mayan People who, often to our delightful surprise, shared with us specific details about their venerable ceremonial and curative ways, practices that are not usually mentioned in archeological or anthropological books. Oral tradition is one particular valuable way of living out the culture in any age, it seems. Occasionally it balances out, or even cancels out, mistruths or misperceptions in some of our history books.

As Creator would have it, we made two new friends, Obéd López, a Mayan, and Maurice Smith, a descendent of the Afro-Caribbean and East Indian Peoples' diaspora. These two fine young men's roots deeply penetrate the Belizean soil. They became our guides, helping us to visit just about every area of the country. But, more importantly,

Maurice Smith and Obéd López of Belize, good friends and guides

they became our friends. Since then I have made three visits to Belize in order to deepen my knowledge of Mayan culture, and each time these two individuals have been most helpful. But often I had to seek the permission of their wives so that they could take time away from work and family in order to help me explore! But, I must say, that they usually jumped at the chance to "take a little break" away from the house and work.

During these trips my privilege has been to visit a number of pyramids: *Altun Ha* ("stone water"), *Cahal Pech* ("place of ticks"), *Caracol* ("snail"), *Xunantunich* ("stone woman"), *Lamanai* ("submerged crocodile"), and several others. Such spiritual sites allow the mind to move backwards in time so as to imagine some of the activities that took place in communities that utilized these stone pyramid complexes. Though nowadays the edifices have taken on the natural limestone and mortar colors of white and gray, I can easily imagine a time long past when they were brightly painted with turquoise and red earth tones, dancers perched on different levels moving and swaying as they sang their time-honored sacred songs. I can almost hear the sounds of the great wooden drums accompanied by smaller *tambores* made from wood and animal skins, bone or clay whistles, and *maracas* (rattles) sounding their rhythms all together throughout the night against a backdrop of high canopy forest.

All of these sacred sites are undergoing restorative procedures that will take a very long time. But, happily, international archeological and restoration teams are helping local Mayans and other Belizeans in their efforts to preserve their national patrimony. Yet even the best of amateur archeologists get tired, especially under a blazing Central American sun. I especially remember one time shouting up to Santos from the grassy area below the tallest of the Altun Ha complex of temples to let him know that I was ready to take his picture on top of the building, but he had somehow fallen asleep on top of the circular sacrificial spot. It took a tourist going up to visit the same place to arouse him so that he could take up his photo pose! I imagine that the ancient Mayans would not have approved of his solar sleep apnia.

A few days later, on the way back from visiting the temple complex of Caracol that lies deep within the jungle, we encountered a large number of weary-looking sunburned soldiers sitting by the side of a mountain road many miles from the nearest town. As these men are part of the British Commonwealth's military protection of a former colony (British Honduras, now called Belize), they were on their way to practice their "war games" in the mountains and jungle. Evidently their vehicle had lost its brakes, causing it to careen into the hillside. Even though everyone was dangerously tossed about, only a few suffered broken bones or had some kind of pain. Due to the accident their communications system was out so they could not call for help. We arrived just as they were about to send two soldiers on a long, arduous journey down that lonely mountain road to look for someone to rescue them.

We were flagged down by a couple of officers who immediately asked our help in this matter of emergency. It was right then that I recognized one of the officers. A few hours earlier in the day we had passed by their military base just outside one of the small villages. Being quite far from the city, and realizing that we did not have a full tank of gas for such a lengthy trip into the jungle and back, I asked if we could buy some from them at their base. The officer in charge was rather snooty in his British accent and seemed a bit prejudiced toward us. So we left right away, wishing we had not even bothered him, and continued on to visit the Mayan temple.

At that moment on the mountainside he recognized us as well. Santos and I, our anger with him somewhat subsided, now felt really compassionate and so we invited him to accompany us. Upon arriving at the base about an hour and a half later, his attitude, and ours as well, had completely changed. Insisting on writing down my address particulars, he kindly sent us over to the officers' mess hall to eat whatever we wanted. Was I surprised about three months later to receive a very official looking letter from Her Majesty's Government thanking us for our kindness in that moment of soldierly need! One just never knows when life's phoenix is going to rise up out of the ashes of dismay or anger to display itself in friendship and appreciation. It turned out to be a good day for us after all.

Ramón

Ramon Nenadich is a true *Boricua*, a native of Puerto Rico. He tells us that he had a vision some time back that let him know he

Delegates, Native Gathering of the Americas, Ustupu Island, Panama, 2000

was to be instrumental in uniting indigenous Peoples. He has come to fulfill part of that vision, I believe, in the last ten years. Both a respected scholar at the University of Puerto Rico at Rio Piedras, San Juan and also an internationally called-for speaker on the perspective of Native concerns of the Caribbean Antilles, he has traveled to the United Nations in Geneva and many other places seeking to share with the world the indigenous vision that he himself has come to know. I connect with his vision and am pleased to be listed among his confreres. Highly regarded by many in the numerous national and international movements that seek to call for and provide for indigenous rights, he pursues, takes in to himself, and lives out a spirituality that is based in the shamanic ways of the People. Because of Ramón I have been able to expand my own indigenous experiences. These, in turn, have helped to validate my sacred work as a priest of 35 years. For me, Ramón is a person well worth knowing who I will always respect as a fellow "people connector." Long may his work continue in defense of the rights of the Native Peoples of this hemisphere!

Kuala

I first met Kuala (Lucindo Gómez) in Panama about eight years ago, a day or so after I had participated in the priestly ordination of a Kuna priest on Tupile Island. Unfortunately, my ride was not there to pick me up at the airport upon my return from *Kunayala* (Kuna Territory), so, in my semi-panic I called a few numbers that I had scribbled down earlier on a piece of paper. On that particular afternoon, Kuala miraculously answered the telephone. He just happened to be present at a special meeting and did not know about me beforehand. Surprised, I am certain, he agreed to meet me later on to give me hospitality in his humble home. I then had a chance to get acquainted with his wonderful family. He has turned out to be one of the most knowledgeable people concerning Kuna culture, and since that first meeting, has opened me up to many adventures among the various tribes of Panama. Through him and a good number of his friends and relatives I have come to know plenty of San Blas Islands folks. These are people who get up early before first light to fish from dugout canoes, later hunt for food on the jungle mainland or tend to coconut and banana orchards, or plant crops, construct amazing dwellings and other serviceable structures without the use of hammer and nails, or upon being asked, just offer a helping hand when communal work is required. Kuala seems to know everyone around, no matter where we travel in the country. Since that first day of acquaintance I am glad to number Kuala and his wife and family among my special friends. I am also proud to be the godfather of his second son, "Father Scott Ian" Gómez.

Giving a statue from my church in Seaside, California, to the Bishop of Metetí, Darién, Panama, 2006

Rubén and Friends

One of the first Aztec dancers that I got to know more personally and still am glad to call a friend is Rubén Lemus. Based for a long time in the Salinas area, over the years he has taught *danza* (Aztec dance) to many folks, both young and old. Time and time again he and his family and companions have come forward to share their danced form of prayer at baptisms, celebrations of the Virgin Mary, liturgical feasts, church festivals, and b*arrio* (neighborhood) non-violence parades. He sings in *nahuatl* (Aztec language) and has always blended together in himself the ancient indigenous heritage along with his Catholic ways and finds no conflict in doing so. Victor Rey, our friend, also dances and locally guides others in their endeavors. He always takes the time to talk and explain the finer points of his culture to whoever is ready to listen. He not only excels in craftwork when making drums and authentic dance regalia but happens to have a most proficient understanding of herpetology. His humility becomes him. Another friend, more like a son, Omar Mercado was very young when I first arrived in the Castroville parish, and is always helpful to me, along with his family. A leader among his peers, he grew up to be an excellent young man, educating himself both formally and informally and then going back to his community as a high school teacher and sharing his native culture with his students as well. Politically aware and always ready to encourage his

With Aztec dancer Rubén Lemus, after Ecumenical Thanksgiving Service, Carmel Valley, California, 1998

Aztec dancers at Easter Mass celebration, Carmel Valley, California, 2003

Aztec drummer at Ecumenical Thanksgiving Service, Carmel Valley, California 1998

Ecumenical Thanksgiving Service, Carmel Valley, California, 1998

Omar Mercado, cultural and justice activist, teacher and Aztec dancer, 2005

Aztec ceremony in Catholic parish chapel, Seaside, California, 2006

Victor Rey and Tarahumara runners, 2008

people, he, too, dances in the Aztec way and is always vigilant in his community for other urban young people who seek ancient learning with a contemporary feel to it. I would not want to forget Nena and Gilbert Sanchez and their wonderful family of dedicated Aztec dancers who have spent many years supporting me by their prayers and dances. I am proud to have been the godfather of their late daughter Lanette. May the sacred drumbeat continue to be heard in every generation!

Sharman

Sharman Haverly, a woman of Shoshone heritage, is one of those specially gifted people who happens to be wonderfully insightful, almost psychic, in her ability to diagnose what is the particular medical condition of animals like horses or dogs. She knows how to care for them and heal them. They just naturally respond to her. I have witnessed the extraordinarily quick recovery of many animals under her prayerful care quite often. Several times she has called upon me to bless a piece of land or an ill horse or a suffering animal. She is a woman of prayer, always focusing herself on good for others. She has really been there for me at some difficult moments of my life and I am glad for this singular favor.

Sharman Haverly, Carmel Valley, California

Sights Seen

Invitations

I have come to realize that a person can fit a lot into a week or two of time. I have done so often. In fact, most of the adventures that I speak of are what I might call brief "friendship missions," trips that had nothing official to do with my ministry as a priest. Rather, they were excursions that I was able to take over the years, usually a week after Christmas or Easter and about three weeks during the summertime. I always base these fun encounters on friendship, and never really plan them too tightly, so that I might be free as each day fully reveals itself to my companions and I. It is a different way to travel, I realize. Most people would rather know weeks or months in advance what airline or hotels they will use and what exact cities they will visit. That is not my usual way. Yes, I do like to see the sights just like everybody else, but I also seek that "extra" experience that is waiting for me somewhere just around the corner, or should I say, just around the bend in the river. Nevertheless, I believe that I do have the hang of it: I know how to travel well in many kinds of circumstances.

Unexpected and unplanned invitations to visit native friends in other countries have really helped me to enlarge my perceptions of life in this world. Like my own father before me, I can review the stamps in my passport: Belize, Brazil, Canada, Colombia, Costa Rica, Cuba, Dominica, Guatemala, Guyana, Mexico, and Panama (not to mention the many states and provinces of North America and European countries) and muse reflectively, calling to mind people and places that the Spirit of God has caused me to experience. For me, each of these official government stamps symbolizes time well spent with good people just like me as far as our humanity goes, but people so very different as far as culture and spirituality go. Every one of these passport stamps reminds me of adventures in jungles, mountains, and towns, villages situated along rivers, lakes and streams, hotels, native style homes: (*casas, palapas, chozas, malocas, chiruatas*) made of thin trees, *bejuco* (jungle vine), and *joron* (palm leaves) and located in the midst of mountains, cliffs, savannahs and jungles.

I have seen my share of anacondas, caimans and crocodiles, giant menacing-looking spiders and piranha fish, sloths, tapirs, capybaras, and jaguars. I have eaten *danta* (tapir) flavored with *ahí* (jungle ants sauce) and almost got to taste monkey meat. I have feasted on fish from the Amazon River accompanied by *cassava* or *manioc* (flat bread made from the *yuca* root). Often I have enjoyed many a good local beer as well. I have been stopped at police and army checkpoints as I entered areas known for narco-trafficking and paramilitary groups. I am sure that the soldiers wondered what this very pale-looking priest was doing with Native friends and guides.

I have passed through many places where for miles around no one even remotely looked like me. Yet in every place I was always made to feel welcome, even though the local accommodation was often quite basic indeed. I have survived heavy jungle rains, flooded rivers, extended dugout canoe trips, high humidity and continuous burning sun. I have visited myriads of islands and have come to be able to distinguish the many shades of green foliage and trees while flying over the jungle in an *avioneta* (small plane). Sadly, I have also travelled airborne over the Amazon tropical rain forest and seen the massive, probably irreparable, destruction caused by fires and mining and logging. *The journey* often takes us onto territory that we oftentimes would not normally desire to visit, but even that is part of *the dream* unfolding in our lives. No *dream*, no *journey*, I suppose.

A Visit to a Shaman

A few months after my father's death, I felt that I needed to get away for a break. His illness and death, the parish work, my writing, and other responsibilities let me know that some kind of respite was necessary. I had various options in mind when a phone call from a friend helped open up the path for me. Looking back on it, I suppose that *the journey* was now taking a different path while *the dream* was still developing within me.

My more recent second visit to Venezuela, at the invitation of the shaman José Luis Piaroa through Santiago Obispo and his lovely wife Nancy Guzmán, truly opened my eyes as to how life is lived in a remote section of the State of Amazonas. After reaching the capital Caracas, my final destination was Puerto Ayacucho, a developing and, it seems to me, overpopulated, frenetic city on the banks of the Orinoco River. Recently many people have come here looking for work, but it seems to me that gainful employment is not that easy to find. The newcomers stay and start their families and so the city grows. The population is made up of native *etnias* (ethnic groups, tribes), *criollos* (mixed Indian, European and Afro-Caribbean heritage), with tourists from around the world or a few visiting *Americano* evangelical missionaries. As a priest I am sensitive to the lamentable evangelical-versus-Catholic syndrome whenever it manifests itself. Some "evangelical" neighborhood *barrios* (neighborhoods) contain individuals who constantly use loudspeakers to play "Christian music" songs at extra high volume for all to hear, whether they want to listen or not. As a local leader in the worldwide ecumenical movement that seeks and works hard for greater Christian unity, I am not always sure about how to think regarding such a tiresome phenomenon. But this is just as much part of the religious reality of contemporary Latin America as it is in the North, I am sad to say.

The Salesian order (S.D.B.) began missionary work here in the first part of the twentieth century. They have a proud tradition of working with the local *etnías* (tribal groups) for many years, always upholding human dignity and indigenous rights, it seems to me. I have spoken with many Salesian missionaries and Native People themselves regarding the development of their approaches down through the years and things seem to be good, all things considered, in a land where many kinds of undesirable flux affecting the lives of the People seems to be commonplace.

Since the early days of Christianity, or any other religion for that matter, proselytism (missionary work) has no doubt always been somewhat of a controversial item, depending if one is on the giving end or on the receiving end of the process, or perhaps even in between. It is really about one group desiring to share what is felt to be important enough to share with another group, often a people dwelling at some great distance. The shareable entity is the group spirituality, the religion. Historically, this religious entity has been contributed from one group to another by various means: attraction without guile or attraction with guile, force, or violence. Many times the intentions were good, but the methods were disastrous. Sixteenth- and seventeenth-century European missionary efforts bear witness to this. Very often during colonial times (note: the word "colonial" comes from the Greek language version of Christopher Columbus's name that is used by Spanish-speaking countries: Cristóbal Colón > *colon*ial, *colon*y, *colon*ize, etc. The various periods of entering Native People's lands, seizing them, and making slaves or servants of the inhabitants are attributed to this "discover" of the Americas), military influence within the sharing culture was also involved or, one might add, over-involved in the missionary process. It was more often than not "cross + sword = missionary effort" instead of simply "cross = missionary effort." Religion was confused with culture and vice versa over and over. The results, we now know, were in actual fact disastrous for the ones (Native People) receiving the religious entity (Christian Faith), as well as for those trying to share that entity (priests, nuns, lay people, ministers). We are all still learning from our mistakes, but perhaps very slowly. Education about the many cultures and sub-cultures is all important for our own time.

At other eras, like the present day, marketing methods taken over from the business or entertainment world appear to be utilized by some of the latter-day more "evangelical" missionaries, as their interpretation of the Christian message instructs them to "save souls from eternal damnation." The biblical command of Jesus to "love one another" in this present reality seems to be sorely lacking as attention is put more on the other-world goal of "heaven." Over the years I have listened to complaints from Native people, other more "human rights and justice centered" missionaries, or even critics of any species of missionary efforts, about the well-intentioned yet ultimately destructive work of groups like New Tribes Mission or the Summer School of Linguistics. Ultimately the People lose. Removed from their sacred ceremonies, they then begin to lose their culture, their language, and ultimately, their history. Without their own way of life and spirituality they readily become displaced, marginalized and, one might say, are turned into "generic Christians."

But I must say that things usually turn out to be different when the People, upon experiencing mutual and lasting true friendship, voluntarily accept the gifts being offered. They in turn will have much of their own spirituality, culture, and well-lived daily life to share with missionaries who also, one by one, will become internally enriched and ultimately transformed by what they also receive from the People. Friendship, I believe, is the key to all of this, no matter when the era occurs in history or who make up the "mission-ized" group. True friendship can carry many a burden, including shareable spiritualities.

I consider two of these Salesians to be outstanding: Monsignor José Luis Davisson, bishop of the Amazon Vicariate, and Father Giuseppe Bórtoli, missionary and respected anthropologist who spent over twenty-two years living with the Yanomani People, speaking their language and living their ways. I know that several times publically he has confronted another well-known but nevertheless controversial anthropologist, Napoleon Chagnon, who he felt was holding forth and teaching false notions about the Yanomamis. Father Bórtoli has been very helpful over the years in explaining to me his personal adventures with the Yanomami and even recognizing the connections between my own studies and his personal experiences with the People of different ethnic groups in the jungle and savannah regions. Indeed, I felt quite pleased when invited to accompany him on a two-week visit to Yanomami territory by means of *avioneta* (small airplane), *bongo* (canoe), as well as trekking along arduous jungle trails. Though I have yet to actually prepare myself for such a journey, I still look forward to it. I know that I would return two weeks later much more fit than when I left (and perhaps many pounds lighter!). For this plan and other aspects of *the* future *journey, the dream* is already being prepared for me by some other fellow travelers, I firmly trust.

The day after my arrival in Puerto Ayacucho I found myself driving a large truck past a police checkpoint towards a Hiwi village in a savannah section of the Amazon. My friends had secured two young guides, Calibrato and Climaco in order to make sure that I

Bishop José Luis Davisson and Piaroa community leader José Otero, Amazon, Venezuela

should arrive safely on my "safari" to the house of the shaman. Though we tried to communicate in Spanish, I came to realize that it was only their second language. It would be much better for me to shut up and just point to things. This method seemed to work. The journey under the burning sun was long and arduous. It was impossible to sit down on the lava-like rocks because they reflected the sun's intense heat, and it was just as uncomfortable to lie on the ground due to biting ants and other insects. The same difficulty was faced when leaning up against a tree. Who knows what kinds of venomous snakes and other assorted and unknown to me critters might descend from above?

I remember that I was carrying a gift of about fifty resplendent peacock feathers for my shaman friend. As they had been passed on to me earlier on, I thought that it was my turn now to gift them to someone else who would appreciate them. What a sight I must have been walking in the jungle with such a strange load! Peacocks are not native to this jungle, so I had thought that they just might be the appropriate gift for him. My companions carried backpacks filled with food and a variety of other gifts. After hours of hiking along an overgrown jungle trail, we finally arrived at the shaman's place.

Was I surprised at the three-storey beehive-looking house that was standing before me! What architecture! What symmetry! Though certainly not what I expected, there it was in front of my eyes. The inhabitants, as perhaps was their custom when speaking to unknown strangers, informed us that he was not at home. Momentarily I thought that I had come on this journey for nothing. But after receiving the customary hospitality drink of water and farina, it was announced that I could come forward to see the shaman. This took me by surprise, for I thought that he was not at home as we had been told. I immediately presented myself, giving him my usual

With two celebrated jungle missionaries, one elderly and the other, the renowned Father José Bórtoli, Amazon, Venezuela

bear hug. Then as he sat on his *chinchorro* (hammock) with the rest of the family gathered around, I began to distribute the gifts. First the foodstuffs from town, like oatmeal, cheese, rice, and chicken; then some of my recently deceased dad's caps and t-shirts. He was really pleased, I could see. Then out came some Indian beadwork and a few other useful items, such as a forehead flashlight and some cloth. His eyes twinkled with surprise as I waved before him a small oriental fan that a friend had given me, and whispered: "*para ceremonias!* (for ceremonies!)."

As evening drew near, we bathed in the river. I thought about piranhas, crocodiles, pythons, and jaguars, but they did not seem to be near at that particular moment. As soon as I went back into the *churuata* (house), José Luis prepared a *yopo* ceremony in my honor. Outsiders often remark that in this ceremony the Natives "talk with the ancestors." I observed him preparing the healing medicine powder, the very same way one of our pharmacists would measure out some medication. Shortly after the participants received their dosage, the shaman took up his *maraca* and chanted for what seemed like an hour or so without stopping for an extended break. I marveled at his ability to do this. I believe that he was singing about the first moments of creation, the formation of individual plants and animals and human beings, the power of his words leading us into the present moment of celebrating Creator's care. Perhaps his songs are a bit like someone else recounting the acts of God remembered within the biblical Book of Genesis and how it relates to us today. In between the singing we sat quietly in our hammocks, remaining alert to everything happening in our physical presence as well as those activities within our inner consciousness. Soon dawn came, and I realized that we had been praying all through the night.

As I recall, it was a good experience and by means of this ancient ritual I was able to see my recently deceased father momentarily appear as young and vibrant, wearing a suit and rolling up a cigarette, as was his custom. He had that debonair look of his and he turned and smiled at me. I felt very much affirmed that he was alive and well and enjoying the heavenly dimensions of life. Yet he was still relating to me as my own Dad. It was good and comforting for me. Among other visions, I also remember seeing lots of disheveled people returning home across a bridge somewhere in Eastern Europe, reclaiming their devastated city. The invaders were crossing back on the other side of the bridge, staring at them with anger. About two weeks later, when back in California, I saw the exact same thing happening on TV. It was a news-clip about Bosnia. I had "seen" this same event happening during the ceremony in the Amazon jungle. It was amazing. It is not easily explainable. As I look back on this ceremony,

Piaroa Shaman Bolivar's churuata (home)

Relaxing in a hammock after hiking to Shaman Bolivar's home, Alta Carinagua, Puerto Ayacucho, Venezuela, 2004

I feel that the Holy Spirit of God showed me both a past event and a future event within the same space of time. I have no other way of explaining it. The ancient medicinal practices of the Amazonian Peoples are as real as our own Western ways of medicine. They are complementary, but different from each other. Both are effective. When correctly led by a legitimate spiritual leader, one has nothing to fear; only healing will ensue.

At other times in Alta Carinagua, one of the Piaroa tribal villages near Puerto Ayacucho, I have been a privileged guest of another important shaman popularly known as Bolivar, perhaps named after the eighteenth-century South American liberator Simón Bolivar. I suppose that his shamanic ranking in the midst of all his fellow tribal shamans is probably that of an "archbishop" of spiritual sages, for he is indeed wise. And yet he is humble.

I might comment that one unusual characteristic of many shamans that I have known, besides their practical curative wisdom, is a childlike spirit accompanied by a readiness to smile or perchance laugh, even in the midst of what an outsider might term a "serious" ceremony. Though we are not usually privy to it, I would imagine that, even during a complex brain or heart surgery in the operating rooms of some of our best hospitals, a certain amount of humor is shared by doctors and staff. Humor, when used well, can always help relieve the pressure of a difficult moment. Wittiness has always been a part of my life, especially that kind which is termed "British humor" with its unique *double entendre* qualities, its double meaning for certain words. Either one "gets it" or one does not. That is the way of humor. We must not take ourselves, or certain aspects of life, too seriously; otherwise we might just miss out on something very important that is going on. For me, humor is a gift of God that should always be practiced, developed. It is crucial part of *the journey*, no less than *the dream*. I have found this to be always so.

Along with his extended family I have shared in his own *yopo* ceremonies as well as an annual blessing-renewal ceremony that takes place at a waterfall deep in the jungle near his home. Other shamans under his tutelage are usually allocated precise amounts of *yopo*. I have even noticed a little child, who seems to have been "chosen" for future shamanic leadership, drawing close during the rites to receive an age-appropriate dose. After a period of meditation each one of these leaders would then proceed to the cascade of water, inviting the local band of men, women, and children to be held under its curative waters momentarily as the spiritual leaders chanted, shaking their *maracas*. Of course, large crystals were peered into ahead of time to "diagnose" any present difficulties and discomforts.

One unusual spiritual *fait accompli* that I was able to set up was an "ecumenical and interreligious" newborn child's blessing ceremony. It took place in Santiago and Nancy's home, being held for their younger child Ruaye. Santiago's own father, an elderly evangelical pastor, participated as well. I am not aware of any other ceremony like it ever taking place. Each in our own way prayed the blessing with water, the bible, sacred feathers, ceremonial cigars, blessed oil, sage, and incense. At various moments hymns were sung by the pastor, as well as ancient indigenous chants led by the shaman accompanying himself with a *maraca* in one hand and a bouquet of plumes in the other. We all shared personal prayers in a variety of languages and blessed the child with water. It was not a baptism, but a different kind of ceremony. As the incense wafted throughout the place, smiles could be detected on everyone's face.

For me, it was indeed a profound celebration of unity in action. Perhaps it is a sign of what might happen when open-minded people of different religions come together to celebrate common spirituality. I hope so. The Sunday following this event was special as well. I attended an evangelical service in Bolivar's Piaroa village. The young minister was from the same tribe. At one point he invited me

With two Evangelical Pentecostal ministers and a shaman one Sunday morning in Alta Carinagua, near Puerto Ayacucho, Venezuela, 2002

to say something to the congregation. I responded by announcing to his congregation that I had come to them carrying the blessings and prayers of the people from my parish back in California. They were really pleased and expressed their thankfulness with applause. I cherish a special photo of the shaman Bolivar, the two evangelical ministers, and myself taken shortly after the service. The ample roof of genuine spirituality and human sharing of the sacred is large indeed! More of us should spend time under it, I would venture to say.

Maria Lionza

There is an interesting religion in Venezuela that has to do with a mysterious person called Maria Lionsa. Her name is a contraction of *Maria de la Onza* (Mary of the Jaguar). This spiritual practice is both nationalistic and somewhat syncretistic, taking into itself elements of European, African, and Indigenous religion. People of all levels of society follow it by prayer, making the appropriate ritual offerings of perfumed plants, candles, fruit, liquor, and inscribing special symbols in chalk on and around an altar shrine made of lots of gathered river stones.

Observing a Maria Lionza Ceremony, Monte Sorté, Venezuela, 2005

The ceremonies are most interesting, for in them a certain man or a woman in the group of worshippers becomes a medium for the activity of sacred personages that now live in the spirit world but who also want to help us here on earth. The helping personages come from the "courts' of the three *potencias* (areas of power). The triad is composed of personages called Maria Lionsa, Black Philip, and Guaiacaipuro. They dwell invisibly on high but are very present in our world as well. Summoned by all devotees in the ceremony, they speak through a man or woman medium who then gives a *receta* (prescription) to the *paciente* (patient) to effect a curative action. All of this takes place in a preferred jungle setting, especially the most famous shrine at Monte Sorte in Yaracuy State or even in neighborhood chapels filled with an abundance of statues of all kinds of official church saints as well as other personages, historic or not. I have witnessed the fervor of the people and, though it is not exactly my "cup of tea," I recognize it as being helpful for many. Until recently I had not even known about it. I am most appreciative to Nancy Guzmán and her friend Flor for bringing me to one of these ceremonies. However, as I indicated, there are elements of this religious way that I cannot quite splice into my own inherited and personal theology. As many of the people claim to be Catholic as well, perhaps a lot of study and extended discussion needs to take place between its devotees and the church leadership within the country. There is much about both culture and religion that many of us do not easily understand; and yet I suppose that this is fine too.

A visit with jungle friends: two sloths, a loro, and a python snake, Amazon, Brazil

A long time ago, in the 1970s, a young Jesuit brother from Spain named José María Korta went to live among the Yekuana Tribe. He

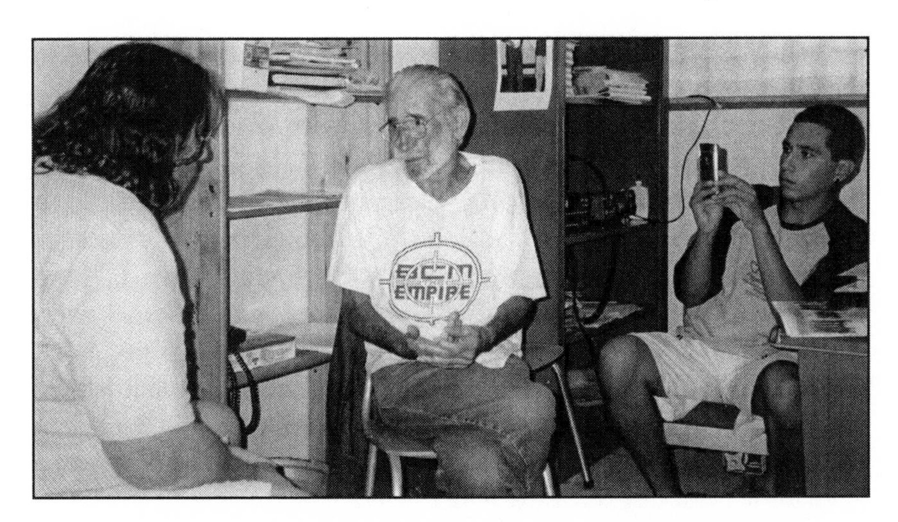

Discussing experiences and new ideas for Native educational opportunities with the controversial Jesuit Brother Korta and seminarian from Peru, Ciudad Bolivar, Venezuela, 2006

totally adapted himself to their culture, even wearing a traditional loincloth daily. As the years went by, he became a kind of advocate for their human rights and later on helped found an intertribal indigenous place of higher learning called Universidad Indígena de Venezuela (Venezuelan Indigenous University) at Tauca in the State of Bolivar. From afar, I admired his work, even though some Venezuelan authorities and a few members of the hierarchy did not like his methods of involvement. Perhaps he was localizing some kind of "liberation theology." It must have had a positive effect. Later on in life he was formally adopted in the tribe and received the name "White Ibis." Such nomenclature, no doubt, relates to his pale skin and white beard. I am glad that I have met him and had a chance to record our discussion about a number of ideas that will promote native rights and educational possibilities in such a remote part of South America in the days to come.

As mentioned earlier, humor has always played a great part in my life, helping me to maintain my sanity as well as giving me a way to exit some difficult situations. Upon occasion it is good to laugh at oneself; it is essential not to take oneself too seriously all the time. I suppose that humor might somehow have a connection with the virtue of humility, something that many of us seem to need most of the time. Perhaps I might offer an example.

I never expected to spend some time with the Amazon State's first indigenous governor, but I did. Liborio Garulla is a man of the Baníva *Etnía* (Tribe), and among his many civic and state responsibilities, he is most concerned with how we should properly manage our world's natural resources, especially the powerful vegetal lung called the rainforest which continually breathes clean air into the rest of our world. A few of us, a Venezuelan, a Kuna, and a Taino, and I, were privileged to make an evening visit to him at his office where we planned to offer him some gifts. For about four days we had been doing some intense planning, along with some Amazon tribesmen from Venezuela, for our next Native Gathering in Puerto Rico; this time we wanted to reach out to the tribes in the Amazon and make them a full part of the proceedings.

Just prior to the meeting, some of us went for dinner. During the last part of the meal, someone suddenly interrupted me as I was lifting up a spoonful of tasty sauce, ready to pour it over some meat. Trying to do several things at once: lift sauce, think, speak, I somehow accidentally spilled a lot of it on my last remaining clean shirt! The next day I was to fly home. "How can I go see the governor now, like this?" I protested. But to no avail. My fellow delegates reminded me that I was both an important spokesperson for our cause and a credible ambassador for what we wanted to ask him to do for us, especially because I was a priest! Not so sure if they were telling the truth or joking with me at that particular moment, I reluctantly agreed, and away we went. Though I attempted to hide the enormous stain by keeping my camera bag over it at all times while in the governor's presence, I am not so sure that it worked. He must really be a polite man because he acted as if everything was normal with me. However he was regarding me from his chair immediately across the room, I felt bold enough on that occasion to invite him to visit California and stay as a guest at my parish house in Carmel Valley. So far he has not been able to come; perhaps at some future time I will get a call from him!

Cooling off in the Rio Frio, Belize, 2001

Belize

I have had some really enjoyable times in the little Central American country of Belize that lies between Mexico and Guatemala; but I also have also experienced some hair-raising moments as well in this tiny nation of diverse and affable people. I will always remember that some true friends, Obed and Maurice, once saved my life on the Rio Frio. One time, after a few days of visiting jungle areas, we decided to take a swim in order to cool off. My companions went over to a deeper section of the fast flowing river where there were plenty of boulders of varying sizes partially submerged in the river, while I went elsewhere nearby to lay down for a spell in some cool shallower water. Soon their boisterous laughter encouraged me to get up and go join them. From their own vantage point they could see the easiest path for me, but from my line of vision, it seemed better to take another watery path towards them. I should have listened to their warning.

All of a sudden the current took me. I was twirled around and around, and yet somehow I was able to quickly grip onto some rocks with both hands and feet, probably looking like a frog stretching out all four legs, attaching them to nearby rocks. At the same as I cried out

Xunantunich, a Mayan Temple, Belize, 2003

in alarm, my buddies immediately jumped into action, thank God. It was a life and death moment for me. For one of the few times in my full life, I felt fearful and close to death. They soon gripped my hands and, heavy though I was, pulled me to safety, all the while the water doing its best to carry me away. Then, after a long moment of silence we began to laugh, and continued our fun. If they had not been there for me at that exact moment, I would have been swept downriver, all of my bones breaking on the rocks along the way. The epithet "Jesus saves" took on new meaning for me at that moment! Such a part of *the journey*, I concluded, should never be part of *the dream*! Nevertheless, friends are indeed wonderful and come in very handy, especially at those truly difficult moments of our lives.

With a young armadillo in Belize, 2003

A couple of days later our group ascended and descended *Xunantunich*, one of the highest of the Mayan pyramids. Obed went ahead of me and I slowly descended on steps that in eons past had been made for feet much smaller than my own. Pretty soon there was nothing for my hands to grip on that ancient wall and I immediately experienced the sense of vertigo. A feeling of panic ensued and I cried out, looking about nervously. Here I was perched half way down a treacherous escalade, stomach to wall, with flat ground many yards below me. It became even more difficult when some French tourists just a few steps above me and oblivious to my predicament, descended towards me very quickly. Almost falling, I once again cried out for Obed. True friend that he is, instantly he was there for me, letting me use his shoulder as a contact point for my left hand. I felt safe and the vertigo left me. It was a close call. Needless to say, as soon as possible we cooled off and recounted our recent days' most harrowing events, each with a fine Belizean beer in hand, our bodies and minds at rest. Individuals, after experiencing a time of bodily or spiritual imbalance, may find it good to internalize the meaning of the ancient but profound greeting: "*Salaam alaykum, shalom aleichem,*" peace be with you! On that particular day my friends and I came to know something more of this peace that comes from on high, a peace that is most shareable.

Carib chief Hilary Frederick, Dominica, Caribbean

Island of Dominica

Hilary Frederick (r.i.p.), a Kalinago, was a special friend of mine. I first met him at the initial Native Gathering of the Americas in Puerto Rico. His Caribbean British accent, unique posture, and depth of knowledge expressed in the presentations made him stand out powerfully among the other delegates, in my opinion. He shared with us his vision of a confederation of Caribbean islands, a "trade winds" kind of confederation, that would allow for the trade and good communications that once existed in ancient times. After the Gatherings we always stayed in touch. One time, several years ago, he invited me to visit Dominica, an island aboriginally called *Waitukubuli* ("tall is her body"), for a special agricultural celebration that was planned for the *Kalinago* (Carib) farmers of the Carib Territory of the island. As he was the Chief, I was to be his special guest. I jumped at the opportunity, cleared my calendar, and ordered the plane tickets.

When I arrived at the airport in the capital city of Roseau, I excitedly and somewhat innocently took a flash picture within the terminal building before every one had been properly processed through the immigration and customs gates. Somehow, in my jet-lagged state I failed to see the "No Photography" sign. Everything stopped in the room, all eyes looking at me. A man who gave the appearance of being bureaucratically official quickly approached, scolding me severely, and asking why I had come to the island. "What kind of welcome into another country is this?" I thought. I quickly informed him that I was a guest of the Carib chief and that seemed to change everything. Now I was a special person! Almost a travelling diplomat! His attitude now more gracious, he quickly processed me and led me out to meet the awaiting Hilary who then brought me up into the Territory.

The Kalinagos are self-sustaining. As tropical farmers, their crops include bananas, cassava, coconuts and a variety of other plants. Though money is scarce for them, they are a People who not only survive, but thrive. The community, distributed in villages with wonderful names like *Salibia, Sineka*, and *Bataka*, is slowly growing, while at the same time it works very hard to maintain the unity of its ancient culture. Their Kalinago ancestors were among those who saw the approaching ships of Christopher Columbus and many of the early Caribbean explorers. Caribs were always great travelers among the islands, trading their goods from large dugout *gli glis* (canoes) and bringing back items from as far west as Honduras and as far south as the Orinoco delta.

Wherever we went on the precious jewel of an island, Hilary was always greeted as "Chief"; and that he was. He seemed to know everyone and everyone knew him. In our many conversations he expressed a great deal of compassion for his people and their future. When we last talked, our conversation revolved around his dream of making a movie about his People. He wanted to take on the role of one of the earlier chiefs. He became, not only my tour guide for the Territory and much of the island, but also someone who shared with me quite a bit of information about island history and present reality of the Caribs.

I really felt at home with his family and friends. His mother made several cups of tea for me the same way my own mother would have prepared it. We had some good conversation as she answered a lot of my questions. Up at the chief's house I was not always so well prepared for early morning outdoor showers taken from buckets of collected rainwater. Invariably, I would somehow manage to be lathering myself up just as the locals would walk past me, heading down the hill so very early in the morning to tend to their farm plots! Oh well, when in Rome (or Dominica for that matter), do what the rest of the people do! Several times we breakfasted on good coffee and fried chicken legs, a local delicacy. After this morning repast I was more than ready to meet the people. Hilary sometimes would ask me to film my interviews, always ready to help with the questioning. Each individual was quite frank with the answers. He seemed especially proud when they spoke clearly of their humble island business practices which allowed them just enough money to sustain themselves. Some of the ancient curative practices like bathing a patient in rainwater containing a heavy mixture of sweet-smelling herbs and petals still take place. I was quite surprised when Hilary handed me a bottle of therapeutic snake oil. I have yet to learn the name of the specific species utilized and exactly how to correctly administer it!

I have a wonderful memory of driving back and forth several times in the same hour on the Carib Territory's main road, the car filled with both the Chief and some young folks who really wanted to advertise the agricultural festival. A portable sound system was devised for their ongoing proclamations at each of the villages, the large loudspeaker of which they had stuck out of the trunk of my rented car. We had a lot of laughs doing it, but I really had to be careful because I was driving on the other side of the road, British style, and had to avoid cement ditches, children, and dogs constantly running across the road.

I became aware of certain signs of the ancient ways: drums, the rattles, songs, *calabash* (gourd) carvings, dugout canoe building, *cassava* bread (although on Dominica it is not served plain as in other traditional cultures but often mixed with sugar or coconut and made into cakes), natural fiber basketry, and a certain amount of remembered Carib words in the daily vocabulary. Hilary's brother was an expert at baking *cassava* flatbread and cakes and I took some home with me. The Karina Cultural Group and the Karifuna Cultural Group dutifully teach some of the ancient ways to youth, not only in Dominica, but also as they travel to other islands of the Antilles as well.

I really enjoyed concelebrating Mass in the Carib Territory. A priest from the neighboring parish usually celebrates a Mass in the morning at a village chapel near the entrance to the Territory and another one in the late afternoon at its other end. In these chapels the altar is actually made of a small canoe held up on two supports. It is a fitting symbol for the eucharist because the canoe was always the only means of travel among islands for visiting or bartering natural foods, whether fish, fruit, or vegetables. Exchange of both words and food were only made possible by means of canoe travel in ancient times. So for these people the canoe is a powerful symbol for the word and food of the eucharist that is spiritually exchanged, or shared, among so many of our world's inhabitants today. Murals on the wall express Kalinago spirituality and history. The drum is used in the liturgy and the congregation sings well.

I remember that the priest spoke his homily, his Sunday instruction, in standard Caribbean English for the first half of it and then plunged directly into *Kweyol* (Creole). When he made the switch it seemed to me that the people then really listened up to his words. With my basic knowledge of French I was able to pick out and understand about every fourth word, so I probably got the gist of what he was saying. I was quite proud of myself at the moment. When he asked me to say something, I made an appeal for Carib vocations so that young folks would consider serving at every level in the life of the Church.

With Ramón Nenadich and participants flying to Native Gathering of the Americas, Ustupu Island, Panama, 2001

A lot of misfortune has undoubtedly happened to the Kalinago People since Christopher Columbus showed up on their island over five hundred years ago, but this indigenous People still lives, and I believe, have a good future ahead. I would like to help connect them with some of the wonderful folks, native and non-native, that I have gotten to know over the years. Perhaps this will certainly come to pass as I reflect more on *the journey and the dream* that is taking place in my own personal life.

Panama

My first visit to Panama was prompted by an invitation to participate in another Indigenous Gathering of the Americas held that year on Ustupu Island in *Kunayala* (Kuna Tribal Territory) in the San Blás Islands region. From the national airport we delegates flew to the other side of the country where we were met by large dugout canoes and taken to the island. I just knew that I was in a beautiful section of paradise when I gazed at the translucent blue sea all around us, the sun glistening through its warm waves which my hands were reaching into.

At a distance I first heard and later saw a flute and rattle welcome dance that the young people were performing for us as we

Celebrating Mass with Kunas and delegates at Native Gathering of the Americas, Ustupu Island, Panama, 2000

Deacon Elquin, young girl, and I at intertribal Mass

Kuna dancers, Tapir Island, Panama, 2007

disembarked. Our Gathering was planned to concur with the fiftieth anniversary of Kuna resistance to the Panamanian government of the time. It was quite a celebration, replete with reenactments of maritime canoe battles as well as dances and dramatic sketches illustrating the Kuna cultural history. As we delegates were both intertribal and international, we also had many things to share with the Kunas, both ceremonially and in a whole lot of other ways. On the fourth day I celebrated an intertribal Mass in the open air with dances and song offerings from many different peoples. Of course, a lot had to be translated between Spanish, English, and Kuna for all to participate fully.

Though many Kunas live in the capital city and other larger towns, they regularly come back to *Kunayala* to refresh themselves culturally and spiritually. Usually an island child stays in *Kunayala* until he or she is about eight years old before they are sent to relatives in Panama City to learn Spanish. At that time the island was filled with an abundance of children, each one repeatedly calling out to us visitors, "Hola! (Hi!)." It was a real joy for me to be around them.

I have returned several times to Panama and never fail to visit one of these islands for at least a day or so. I love to respond to such invitations because they are one way that we human beings can make, or even deepen, our friendships. One time I was invited to the priestly ordination of a Kuna man named Elquin Nuñez Miró. Going to a small and isolated tropical island for an ordination is not on most people's tourist agenda. But I just had to be there! It was a part of *the journey* that *the dream*ing told me to do. I was being led from within.

Flying into Panama City is spectacular. Tall buildings crowd the edge of the land as it touches the waters. It looks like a petite San Francisco or New York. Off in the distance one can see lots of mountain greenery made up of various kinds of palm trees, along with those that give us bananas, coconuts, mangos, and papayas. There are also hundreds of other kinds of trees, bushes, and plants that produce fruits that we have yet to experience and name in our own particular land of abundance.

My next activity was to seek out and enter a small puddle jumper plane that taxies visitors to the islands. The San Blás area of Panama

Chicha Ceremony, Ustupu Island, Panama, 2000

has over 300 islands, most of them having been lived on and fished from for thousands of years. They are like little spots of green in a huge sea of blue. The plane touched down on the landing strip on the edge of the mainland and at that early hour of 7 AM I entered a motorized dugout canoe, only to be greeted by the very man who was to be ordained, calmly smiling, wearing some kind of French Foreign Legion-looking cap, and hugging everyone as we entered that precarious water vehicle. It was quite a sight to behold.

In about ten minutes we were greeted by a lot of excited people and more of the young folks dancing while playing large pan flutes and rattles. I also felt like I was coming home. My bamboo-like reed dwelling contained a hammock and the kinds of items that would make any weary traveler feel at ease. By then it was about 8:30 AM. While preparing for whatever might be needed by me in the ordination ceremony, I was visited by a group of children, curious to know all about where I had come from. Speaking in Kuna with a little Spanish added in, they took me by the hand and directed me outside to the plaza where the preparations for the 10:00 AM ceremony were being made.

As I was gently pulled along the narrow streets, folks greeted me once again with "*Hola*" ("Hello!") on their lips. You cannot be a stranger for very long on a small island. The women were

Kuna women, Tupile Island, Panama, 2000

With Kuna tribe children, Tupile Island, Kunayala, Panama, 2001

Sharing some words with Kuna elders, Ustupu Island, Panama, 2000

resplendent in their red decorated kerchiefs and *mola* (delicately hand appliquéd cloth) blouses and wrap-around skirts. Most had a piece of refined gold inserted into their nasal septum. Wrappings of small beads adorned their arms and legs. Individually and together they really are an amazing sight. A matriarchal society from time immemorial, they seem to be a people who know peace and mutual cooperation, and it seems to work well for everyone.

The ordination ceremony took place outdoors by the town square. In the bilingual liturgy the bishop, Monsignor Carlos María Ariz Bolea, seemed quite comfortable making some cultural adaptations. Traditional songs and dances were woven throughout the ceremony. Though it was a spectacular event, I was suffering still from the effects of jet lag and needed to go to my comfortable hammock for a nap. A short time later I was summoned to see the bishop at the priest's house for a little celebratory repast.

Luckily I had brought some jars of Castroville marinated artichokes and some wine as gifts which I sent ahead with the children. When I arrived at the humble feast the bishop was already sampling them. He and his clergy friends were most hospitable. I remember him telling me within the hearing of the guests that I did not look like a priest, but that by my bearing I was a real priest indeed. Well, that compliment really hit me well! We then chatted for a while and he made sure that I had my chance to taste some vintage tequila someone had brought for the occasion. Shortly after this he suggested that I take a sabbatical in his diocese, more particularly in *Kunayala*, so that I could get to know his favorite people better. Needless to say, I glowed within. The next day I left the island with that certain feeling of wanting to linger among friends just a little longer, but I had to move on. There was more of *the journey* to make, prompted by my inner *dream*. It is good to give invitations and it is good to receive them. One never knows what amazing adventures are possible during this wonderful gift of life until an invitation is actually given or received. It is like a sacred enticement to savor, just a small portion at a time, some aspect of human pursuit like exploration, friendship, or even just plain old fun.

Another time, after passing through several military checkpoints, some Kuna friends and I went deep into the jungles of the Darién section of the country, not that far from Colombia. It is a danger zone as well. Terrorists, narco-traffickers, paramilitary groups and others have preyed on its indigenous and *criollo* (mixed heritage) population over the years. Once in a while certain people, especially if they have the wrong political connections or are people of some wealth, are found to be missing or kidnapped. Besides all this, the jungle is not the most inviting place for most of us. Some of the most poisonous snakes like the *fer de lance*, not to mention crocodiles, keep the usual tourists at a safe distance. But I am not a tourist! I am a *journey*er! Usually I travel with a knowledgeable local Native friend or two to guide me and ensure my safety. This particular time my plan was to visit the Emberá and Wounan Peoples.

Along the way we took some time to visit the new bishop of Darién Diocese, Monsignor Pedro Joaquin Hernandez Cantarero. A humble man, and obviously pastoral, he spoke of various kinds of constituents living in and around the diocese that he cares for spiritually. From Indigenous People to Afro-Caribbeans to *criollos* to business people recently moved into the area, not to forget the above-mentioned terrorists, paramilitary groups, and narco-traffickers, he knows he needs to reach out to all of them in some way. Once back in California we later sent him a contemporary sculpture of the Holy Family of Jesus, Mary and Joseph for his remote chapel-turned-cathedral. Perhaps it will be a good sign to all of his constituents about the value of family life in all of its forms.

The Darién area is the ancestral home of the Emberás and the Wounan, two related tribes. They have, over many generations,

A jungle sloth and I, Darién, Panama, 2007

learned not only to survive but to live harmoniously with the jungle, constantly respecting its ways. Even though in the last century they were invaded by the horse culture, now they have to deal indirectly with the onslaught of the truck culture as many small roads leading off the nearby Panamerican Highway allow squatters to encroach on their homeland. Though very different from their Kuna neighbors, they cooperate with each other as much as possible, especially because right relationship with each other always replicates right relationship with the sacred land, the body of Mother Earth.

Several times I have spent the night in their homes, ate their food, brought home with me their exquisite crafts as gifts, and even had my body painted with their traditional geometric designs. I feel at home with them. They live in houses that are one storey off the ground. There are no windows, only a roof. Hammocks brought down at night allow the whole family to sleep comfortably until sunrise. More often than not the torsos of the women are left bare and painted with *jagua* (a dark vegetable dye that, when dry, looks like a tattoo). As this kind of paint lasts for weeks on one's body, the areas for painting need to be chosen carefully if one is to go beyond their jungle homeland. I experienced this first-hand. The day after the painting of my body with the most exquisite of symbolic designs, I had need to visit the bishop of Colon-Kunayala in order to help some Kuna elders apply for some financial help to repair the motor

After being ceremonially painted by Emberá women, Darién, Panama, 2007

of their island's communal boat. Little did I realize until after the visit that some of the painted design was showing above my collar and on the end edges of my shirt sleeves. The bishop most likely noticed it; however, being a real gentleman, he was nice enough not to make a comment. I think he knew where I had last been. Maybe he had similar experiences earlier in his own life. I will never really know for sure.

Their music is fast paced and always joyful. The men in their preferred red, blue, yellow or green colored loincloths, the women wrapped in their own multicolored skirts, the dances go on and on. Smiles and laughter express their great joy at moving their feet on the body of Mother Earth, letting her know that her children are near. Appreciating any gifts that I bring from afar, their children wait patiently in line to receive any candy or little toys that I usually bring. How different this is from the attitude of many of our children reaching all at the same time to grab something, sometimes pushing and shoving, lest they miss out. For the first time in their known history, one of their villages boasts a *caciqua* (a female chief) who, not only is a woman, but, as she is educated in the dominant culture also, is especially able to deal with those outsiders who want to take away their ancestral lands. This particular Embera village that I visited, called *Ipetí,* was close to another land-based group of Kunas at *Kuna Ibedi* (similar spelling, different pronunciation), a totally distinct culture. On a first visit to their village, these Kunas treated me to a most exotic breakfast of iguana eggs and a drink of strained bananas mixed with..., well, I do not really know. Mmmm, but it was delicious!

The Ngobe Buglé People are situated more in the north of the country close to Costa Rica. Their women wear long, brightly colored homemade dresses that reach to the ankle while the men wear similarly colored shirts, much like a modern North American powwow ribbon shirt. From roots and tree fibers they make the most excellent of bags, nets and baskets. They are true artists with the sewing machine. The men make the beadwork: necklaces, bracelets, and special bags. They prefer to walk long distances, often with the men in front and the women and children in a single file close behind. Time seems to flow differently for them than for the rest of us so used to our technological environment. I am told that they are the last to gain their own *comarca* (territory) from the Panamanian government only a few years ago.

I have noticed a kind of shyness in many of these folks from upper Panama whenever I have been around them. They are not as immediately accepting of strangers as perhaps are some other tribes. This might be because over the many years they have not been able to trust outsiders and have often suffered greatly under them. In driving through their traditional territory one time, I noticed that the hills were not as full of jungle fauna and flora as in the southern part of the country. My friend then recounted to me that over a hundred years ago international companies like Nestlé had much of the jungle cut down to make room for cows which would then produce milk for their famous chocolates. Now the Ngobé Bugle hesitation to talk with strangers began to make more sense to me. Somewhat nomadic, in these times they often help to harvest coffee on the *fincas* (farms) so as to financially make ends meet.

Costa Rica

I have only visited Costa Rica one time in 2006, but I plan to go back as soon as possible. Prior to my visit, I had originally met Ali García Segura, a member of the Bribri Tribe, during one of the Gatherings in Puerto Rico. He is a published linguist always working on behalf of his people at the University of Costa Rica in San José. I had wanted to learn something of this country's Native People and I knew that he would be of help. With Ali and some colleagues I toured the anthropological department and for later perusal made note of certain books in their library.

An anthropologist friend of his named Daniel Rojas had provided part of my ride from the Panamanian border to San Isidro. Along the way we discussed something I found to be quite fascinating. Many times, in various places in the Costa Rican jungle, one may come across perfectly round stone spheres two to three feet in diameter made by an ancient people. The stones seem to have been prepared in places relatively distant from their discovery sites. Not much is known about them or the culture that produced them. Perhaps they were set up in special alignments. Nobody really knows now because most of them have been moved from their original sites and distributed throughout the country.

One encounters fascinating things when one travels. Ancient gold work from the tribal past is also amazing to see. The People knew how to purify this most precious metal and make wonderful things with it, especially sacred items. Many pieces now preserved in museums seem to me to portray shamanic visionary flights. Often bats, harpy eagles and jaguars were formed out of this precious metal and then put to ritual use for the sake of the People.

Recently at one of the Gatherings in Puerto Rico, I had an opportunity to get to know Fredy Enrique Ortega Jarrin, one of four thousand people in the Cabecar Tribe who speak their version of the exceedingly ancient Chibcha language found in various places in Mesoamerica. He excels in singing traditional songs and has a wonderful way of bringing all of us together to share in his People's dances. In knowing him, and watching him sing with a rattle shaking in his hand, I can sense his connection with the ritual past of all the Costa Rican tribes. The old ways have not really gone; they are very much present in the contemporary life of the People, if only one would take the time to respect and to study their time-honored activities more deeply.

Brazil

Three trips to Brazil, and many phone calls and emails afterwards, make me even more desirous of spending some more valuable time in Brazil; to be circuitously specific, anywhere within its *Amazonia* region. But I am not opposed to getting to know inhabitants and fauna and flora of other areas as well, especially if I will have the pleasure of meeting such wonderful people as I have in the past. On the first trip there were several of us: Santos Cortes, Louis Oropeza, Santiago Obispo and Nancy Guzmán with their little boy Huaykuni, and yours truly. We all rendezvoused in Manaus and hired a truck-like vehicle, the only one available to us at the time. It necessitated a couple of us to take turns riding in the back with our luggage, constantly exposed to the sun. Luckily, since I was the only official driver, this debilitating activity did not apply to me.

Manaus is a large city near the confluence of the Rio Negro and the Rio Solimoes (Amazon River). Besides the usual sightseeing and nature exploring, we had planned to connect with Native communities along the way. After inquiring at various native organizations located in and around the city, we received lots of help. For instance, in a Native owned indigenous handicrafts shop called *Yakino* we met, as chance would have it, a couple of the Indigenous actors who had starred in such movies as *At Play in the Fields of the Lord* and *Medicine Man.* They were friends of its owner, Ismael Pedroso Moreira, also an actor and author, who is quite knowledgeable about many of the tribes of the greater Brazilian Amazon. His information was most invaluable for us and because of him we came to know some Desana Tukano families at Tupé on the river to the northwest of Manaus.

Domingos Savio Veloso Vaez is the *cacique* (chief) in this village and his brother Raimundo Veloso Vaez is the *pajé* (shaman). They and their families experience the daily encroachment of tourism from some nearby resorts that have recently been built. They seem powerless to limit the growth. Who knows how long they will be able to maintain their own special way of life? After explaining some aspects of their unique culture to us, they invited us to share a meal and some further discussion. Our first visit was brief, and even though we were invited to spend the night with them and share in some kind of welcoming ceremony, we had to return to the city before dark. But I sensed that, on this part of *the journey*, as silently instructed by *the dream*, a good connection was being made for future activities. One step at a time, I thought.

Santo Daime

It seems that throughout Brazil there are many adherents of the *Santo Daime* (Holy Gift) way of life. Prior to my visit I did not really know anything about this now international movement which has its origins deep within the Amazon rainforest. The name has to do with the sacred gift of *ayahuasca*, a vine that contains hallucinogenic properties and which is prepared as a medicine for ingestion during ceremonies that take place from evening until dawn, following the time-honored indigenous way. The history of this movement tells me that a blending of Indigenous, African, and European spiritual practices has taken place. In their prayerful worship services, whether in a chapel-like atmosphere or a larger place where several hundred folks are gathered, the women sit together, forming a half-circle, while the men take up the other half. This symbolizes both unity and complementary balance. A central altar is star-shaped with six points, not unlike the *mogen David*, the star of the David, and the medicine, liquid *ayahuasca*, is placed on it. The *maraca*, the rattle, is their main instrument, usually backed up by two amplified guitars. The songs are ballad-like, very repetitive, and easy to follow. They sing of joy, the beauties of God's creation, the jungle forest and all that is alive within it, the purity of the Virgin Mary, the saving action of Jesus. It seems to be a "praise and healing" ceremony. Swaying and dancing in place make up for long periods of meditation during which time the natural exotic sounds of the jungle predominate. Most participants wore black and white clothing, while some touted special insignia or emblems that looked rather like Old West sheriff badges, indicating some kind of rank in the movement. Joy is always prevalent and really obvious on the faces of all the participants. "What were their thoughts throughout the all-night vigil with the medicine?" I wondered. Were they praising Creator for life itself? Were some worried about problems back at home? Were they praying for friends? Were some just caught up in a beautiful experience? I for one experienced the sensation of being jaguar-like, walking a jungle trail continuously upwards, always moving towards a cloud of light at the top of a mountain. My hands, moving to the rhythm of the *maraca* seemed like a set of jaguar's paws. Not being privy to the actual thoughts and feelings of the others present, I knew nonetheless that we were united in our individual experiences. God was more than close to us in this our common prayer. The opening

Santo Daime Cross, Manaus, Brazil, 2003

and closing orations seemed to be taken from a traditional Catholic format. Utilizing a special kind of calendar for planning their events, the devotees are one in prayer both nationally and internationally. I envision that the participants are also naturally oriented to be ecumenical, or even inter-religious, for their unique spiritual movement appears to enjoy continuous growth. Always ready to talk about the meaning of what they do at one of these ceremonies, they are a welcoming group, I must say.

I would be interested to know how the Brazilian Catholic clergy view this phenomenal religious movement since many of its devotees are also Catholic. We know that *ayahuasca* and other plants have been appropriately utilized for millennia in South America for both healing and, to speak of another way of communication, worship of God. In our modern preoccupation with official pharmacological medications versus improper drug use within our contemporary culture, we most likely cannot make room for the spiritual use of plants like *ayahuasca*. Our European religious heritage could never really understand it, I am sure. But I surmise that over the years since first contact, a good number of missionaries without a doubt do understand because they have gotten extremely close to the very people they serve and have been present in the ceremonies. A few have told me so.

After intertribal ceremony near Manaus, Brazil, 2003

Some day I would love to observe an official dialog between the two groups as to the use of *ayahuasca* and the like in worship. Such serious study, controversial though the topic may be, would probably give new meaning to the well-known modern church phrase, "acculturation in the liturgy." My friends and I felt quite thrilled to have witnessed such a ceremony, though we were very tired in the morning. It revealed to us another hidden part of the modern Brazilian experience that is not very well known to visitors. However, I will leave the exploration of this topic to the theologians and practitioners; like a lot of sensitive subjects that might compromise doctrine in some way, perhaps for the time being it is better to allow it some "benign neglect."

Healing a Shaman

My second visit to this amazing country was much more fruitful for me and really quite memorable. When Santiago and I arrived from Manaus once again unexpectedly at their tiny village of Tupé, a few of our friends seemed to be waiting to greet us on the river beach, by some secret means knowing that we were on our way to them. I felt like I was coming home. I could not wait to see Raimundo, the *paje*, the shaman. Perhaps he saw us in vision and told them to be ready. I am not sure. We came in peace and we came bearing gifts. But I did not have even an inkling of the gift that we were to receive in return.

The year before, Santos and I and a number of others had been gathered inside a *maloca*, a Native house, situated in a remote place on the outskirts of Manaus for what I might call, for lack of better words, an "Amazonian intertribal ceremony." Raimundo was the presider. Some of the women present were Santo Daime enthusiasts, another man a follower of Guaraní tribal traditions, and the rest of us were visitors. A small fire centered us as we gathered around. Everyone was encouraged by the songs, the sharing of several kinds of medicines, the smoking of a sacred pipe, the dances and the many personal prayers which were offered out loud in our different languages. Most had to do with peace in our world and healing for individuals. I especially liked dancing barefoot around the fire,

Showing how to build a sweat lodge at Tupé, near Manaus, Brazilian Amazon, 2006

always going clockwise, ritually holding the pipe in my left hand. I am reminded of Kevin Costner in the movie *Dances with Wolves* doing a similar dance of happiness around his fire. But at times, when all of us were moving together, it was a bit difficult since the ground was somewhat uneven. My only preoccupation was the height of the fire's flames and what seemed to me to be a low lying roof. Since the shaman was officially in charge, I did not really have to be overly-concerned. Though the ceremony lasted many hours, no one was very tired or bored. When we took time to be silent, the creatures of the rainforest sang to us.

Though I must admit that this kind of worship activity is not for everyone, it seems to touch something deep and perhaps primeval in those folks who are privileged to be present. It is sincere worship, and not pretentious. It is helpful for many whose daily environment is more technological and urban. I would suggest that the churches could benefit much from studying or reevaluating these ancient forms of joyful worship. After all, they are really part of our own ancient hidden heritage.

But let me return to our arrival on that second visit. After ascending the stairs cut into the sandy escarpment, and upon entering the area of the *malocas*, I once again encountered the shaman Raimundo, this time smiling up at me from his seat on the ground. But something was different. Pretty soon I noticed he was suffering from a large abscess on the inner part of his leg, somewhat near the ankle.

Author in ceremony for healing Shaman's abscessed ankle

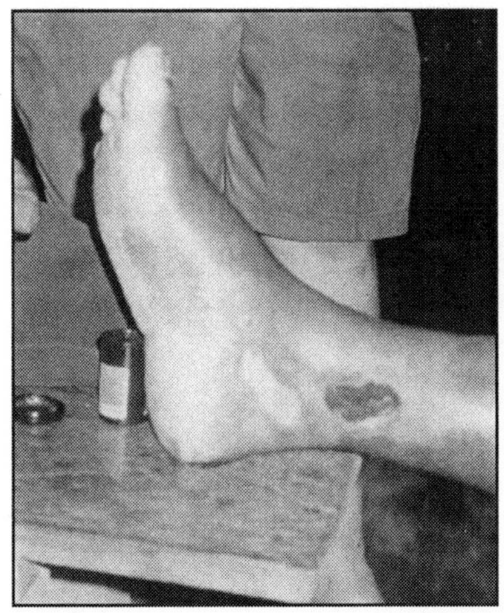

Abscess

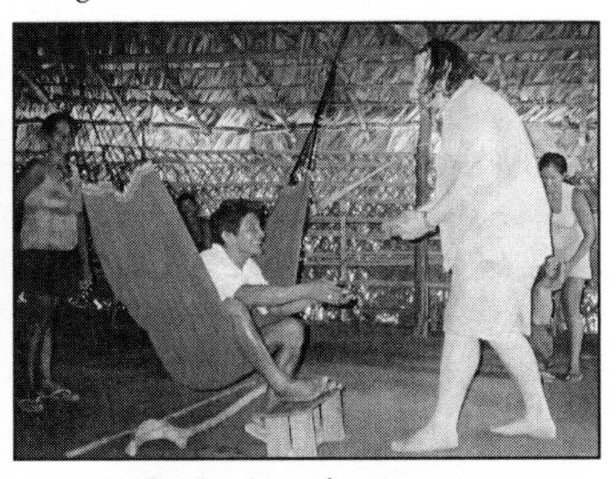

Beginning of ceremony

Showing Shaman's son how to massage ankle to ensure good blood flow

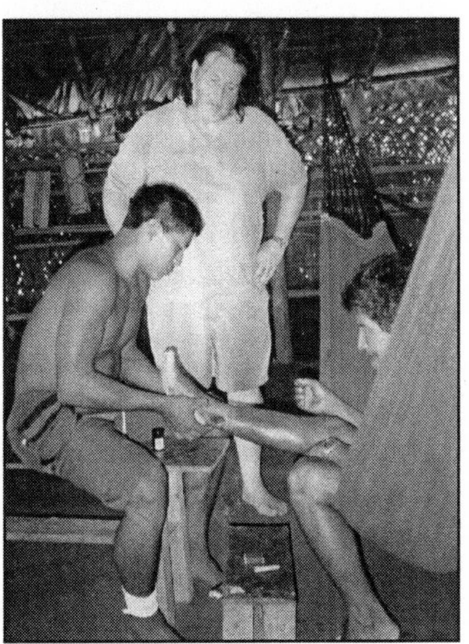

Massage

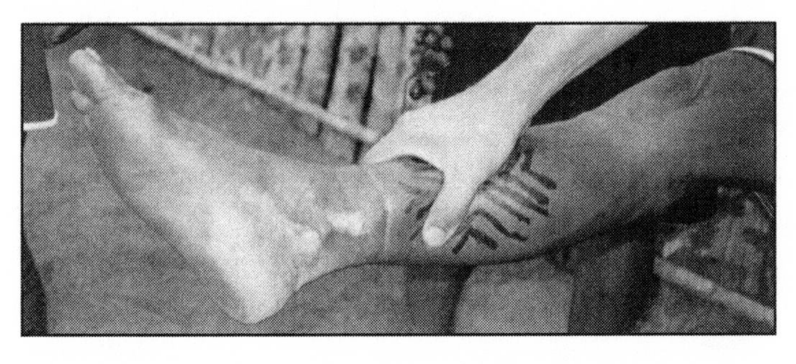

One year later: proof of the healing, near Manaus, Brazil, 2007

To me it seemed to be caused by some kind of insect or snake bite; or as he would consider, it was due to someone else trying to do him harm, as in an evil spell. He greeted me as usual and, after some translated preliminary conversation from Spanish into Portuguese and back again, I offered to pray for him, to anoint him with holy oil. He immediately agreed since he and his family also are Catholics.

I called for some oil and requested that Raimundo be seated in the middle of his hammock. It is usual in most Amazonian ceremonies that a special kind of cigar is smoked during any kind of ceremony. At one point in the ritual the burning part is carefully placed in the mouth, smoke is then being forced through the other end so as to be directed over the patient's head and other parts of the body. Since a ceremonial cigar had been handed to me by someone at that moment, I complied with this Amazonian rite, proceeding with the laying on of hands and the anointing. All during this time his family had formed a circle around his hammock. When we were finished with the prayers, I instructed his son how to massage the area around the sore to allow for better blood flow, asking for this to be done four times a day. I felt a bit like a doctor giving out a prescription.

On my third visit to him a few months later he rejoiced to tell me that he had gotten better very quickly. I felt happy. Here was an example of two ancient ceremonies, each coming from a different world of spirituality, being brought together to make something good happen for someone. But it is really about prayer and one's reliance on the constant care of Creator. Each one of us, no matter who or where we are, can at any moment, reach into the pot of God's healing love and, after having shared in it ourselves, can then begin to share it out.

A third visit to the village was brief, but quite worthwhile. The whole family showed us a large new *maloca* they had built for the purpose of entertaining the tourists. Though we were not tourists to them by now, they wanted to show their appreciation by sharing some music and dance with us before our meal together. Immediately they took up their pan flutes and played a beautifully haunting melody while at the same time everyone, including little children, danced to it in that typically Amazonian style of following the leader in a circle or spiral formation while simultaneously stamping the left foot in rhythm as they move.

Then they brought out two instruments that looked like large jungle megaphones. These gave out the most profound bass sounds while their players danced, stamping their left feet on the packed sandy floor. Even the ground vibrated beneath us. Luckily, I was able to capture this dance on my camcorder. With colorful parrot feather headdresses, beaded necklaces and armbands, and everyone painted with tribal designs and smiling happily, it was indeed a sight to behold and commit to memory. These unique instruments are never shown to tourists because they are sacred, ritually expressing, according to their ancient mythology, something of the long ago first sounds of God's primeval creation. When I heard this, I recalled the Genesis stories of creation and I made the connection. Shortly thereafter we feasted with them.

A Massacre

A few days earlier we had driven north from Manaus to a town called Presidente Figueiredo where we met a family of Swiss immigrants who welcomed us. Their house was in the architectural style of their European homeland, but somewhat adapted to the jungle climate. Nowadays they also raise bees. Having come here in the 1960s to be of service to the Natives of the area, their home was filled with years of documentation about their work. Sadly, they recounted to us about a bomb that many years before had been secretly dropped on a Native village not too distant from us in a remote area of the jungle. A few newspaper clippings that they brought out for us proved their point. Evidently, the government and some multinational enterprises had made plans to build a dam for electricity and they wanted no opposition to their plans. In a more distant time this kind of atrocity was perhaps acceptable to some people and so there was no huge outcry at the time, either nationally or internationally. I was reminded of a scene in the movie, *At Play in the Fields of the Lord,* where the protagonist is contemplating doing a similar kind of atrocity at the bidding of a government official. Perhaps this was the inspiration for the movie's scene. Who knows? I do know that because of their work in this regard there were times when the family feared for their own safety.

On our third trip to Brazil, Santiago and I decided to revisit a few of the places that had been previously seen as well as branch out to other, more distant areas of the Amazon region. There is just so much to see and experience and so little time to do it all! But *the journey* must continue *and* so must *the* guiding *dreams*!

Two Bishops, A Priest, and a Prophet

Once again in Boa Vista, through friends we were invited to meet Dom Roque Paloschi, the new bishop of Roraima. He is slender, in his early forties, and loves to smile and give hugs. As soon as we met him he wanted to know if we would accept his hospitality by staying at his residence. Then, in his older model car, he drove us to a meeting at which he was to speak to those nearby who work among indigenous folks. Once arrived, we could see that he was immediately popular. I know that he will serve the people well. But he will have a tough time because the diocesan finances are severely limited and the needs many, especially for the Native population which he serves. I feel that the mining companies and *garimpeiros* (itinerant jungle miners) close by will not want to work with him, but rather against him. In a place where at times people like Chico Mendes are killed for their work on behalf of human rights or to save the rainforest and all of its inhabitants, I fear for this bishop and others similar to him. He is always in my prayers because such leaders are very important in the work of justice and human rights.

With Roque Paloschi, new Bishop of Boa Vista, Roraima State, Brazil, 2006

On my second and third visits I met up with Father John Clarke, a missionary from Northern Ireland. He is someone I am very impressed with, not just because we are close in age and heritage, but for another reason. On his first stint in the country he contracted leprosy. Though he was cured of it, the effects of this dread disease remain in his leg. He then immediately returned to work with his beloved native population in and around Boa Vista. He is his own person and successful in what he does. We have had some brief but powerful conversations covering many topics. I am really impressed with someone like John who leaves the comfort of his own home to share his presence and life with people far away, to learn from them in return, and to celebrate a common divine destiny. May his spiritual tribe increase, as may the tribes that he serves!

From Boa Vista we journeyed back to Manaus and further on to the village of Tupé to see our Desana Tukano friends once again. This time I shared with them the Crow sweatlodge ceremony. Even though they live in what is for the average traveler an eternally hot environment, they welcomed the opportunity to involve themselves in such an international, intercultural, and intertribal ceremony. The shaman Raimundo and his sons helped us construct the lodge. Once inside, they shared their own spiritual songs, accompanied by *maracas*. I wonder what they were each thinking throughout the time together in this tiny "jungle chapel" juxtaposed with the vast Rio Negro. This particular ceremony also accomplished a healing and reconciliation between two brothers who were at enmity with each other. Beforehand, their families felt that they had to take sides. But things did get back to normal. You just never know when Creator's love is going to take care of things!

Venancio Kamiko is someone that I started to hear about through Santiago. He was born into the Baníva Tribe (same tribe as the present governor of Venezuela's Amazon State) and lived in and around the Rio Negro from the middle of the nineteenth century until his death somewhere near Manaus in 1903. Like Wovoka, the North American prophetic seer who began the late 1800s Ghost Dance movement which highly influenced the hopes and dreams of many tribes during a most difficult period of their history, somewhat earlier on Venancio was also to develop a similar intertribal following along the rivers of the Amazon Basin, in both Brazil and Venezuela.

During that time the influence of Portuguese and Spanish speaking traders, woodcutters, and rubber tree tappers was unashamedly destructive for the tribes who lived along the Basin's many river tributaries. Not only was it socially hurtful for them, but it was also equally destructive because of the introduction of new diseases like measles and smallpox that the People had never before experienced. Venancio, according to all reports, was a "poison finder," who instructed people in each village to put away their witchcraft, to come together in festivals where *caxiri* (manioc beer) was drunk during the festivities, and a form of baptisms and marriages were celebrated. Dances were a great part of these ceremonies. His son, Uétsu, assisted him and later carried on his work. It was to become a millenarian movement, predicting that the People would flourish and not be burdened by the Whiteman's systems of injustice. It also just happened to be a mixture of Catholicism and native religion that was suited to the needs of many folks.

As Santiago and I reached the town of Sao Gabriel da Cachoeira, I became more conscious of Venancio Kamiko's lasting influence. Through reading and visiting with people, I realized that he is still very much venerated. Some time later Santiago actually visited with some of his descendants. He proposed to me that soon together we should write a book about this prophet-seer-messiah kind of person. I agreed, also offering to have a statue carved to remember Venancio Kamico as the important historical figure that he is and to have it placed somewhere in one of his Amazon descendants' indigenous communities where all might see it and remember him. We have begun some work on this project already through interviews and photos taken with his relatives. I have even asked my Puerto Rican friend, José Ortiz, who excels in carving his wooden *santos* (small statues of saints carved in a sixteenth-century Spanish style) to participate in the project. We hope that our final work will be published in English, Spanish, Portuguese, and perhaps in the Baníva idiom.

In this same town, an idyllic place on the Rio Negro where large rapids cause interesting swirls of water to form and re-form constantly, happenstance caused us once again to run into Ismael, our Tariana Tribe friend from the Yakino shop in Manaus. And it was lucky for me that we did, for soon I was enrapt in listening to him, somehow actually understanding what he was saying, as he recounted to me origin stories of some of the tribes now dispersed throughout the Amazon Basin and the Caribbean. The miracle of it was that he was speaking all the time in Portuguese as I was communicating back to him in Spanish. Understanding is accomplished best when two hearts are speaking to one another frankly and in truth. There is not much need of further translation at that moment, I suppose, for later on there will come other opportunities, complete with dictionaries and books of orthography if necessary.

I am simply amazed when I experience what I call "bouts of happenstance." When they will occur is totally unpredictable, but when they do it is magical, or should I say Spirit-influenced! For me, happenstance means that some of life's events, one after another, are somehow connectable for the one undergoing the experience. Meaning for these connected events comes through because it simply makes sense to the person undergoing that particular bout, even though it is often not easily explainable to others at the time. I hope that I am not alone in this! If I may further the use of this example with Ismael, none of us could have easily planned to see each other in this isolated place deep in the Amazon without first having been in communication with each other ahead of time. But we had not done this. Since our first meeting, each one of us wanted to stay in contact, but somehow we were not able do so because we got caught up in our own individual busyness. But the desire to do so was always there, I am sure, even though a time and place were never determined by us. And yet mysteriously we met there in Sao Gabriel da Cachoeira. It is a little bit like old friends from an earlier part of life somehow, by means of other folks, work, vacation, school (or even internet search), find each other and re-connect as if time had not really passed by. These things have happened to me throughout my life and I am grateful for them when they do occur.

That same day, just a few hours later, I was truly surprised and very much pleased to meet the current bishop of this part of Brazil. His name is Dom José Song Sui Wan, a Salesian priest born in China, who is now called to serve as a shepherd in the Amazon. What a *journey* he has already taken in his life, one that he probably never *dream*ed of ahead of time. After welcoming me and showing me around his diocesan residence connected to the church and mission grounds, he brought me out to the gardens to meet his pet. "To meet

Bishop José Song Sui Wan and pet tapir, Saõ Gabriel da Cachoeira, Amazon, Brazil, 2006

his pet! How strange!" I thought. I was thinking that it would be some kind of a cat or dog. No, it turned out to be a tapir, a vegetarian jungle animal with an elephant-like snout and a tight well-packed body not unlike that of a domestic pig. It was tame and seemed to follow him everywhere. I was delighted to finally encounter such an animal that I had only seen in photos and in Mel Gibson's somewhat controversial movie, *Apocalypto.* You just never know who or what, man or beast, that you are going to run into in a remote spot in the Amazon!

Even though at times one might have need to recall the epithet "expect the worst but hope for the best," I have concluded in my own life that it is good not to plan one's life too tightly or too specifically, but rather to always be ready for surprises. The anticipation alone signifies to me a kind of openness to the future, an openness that is positive and ready to accept whatever comes along. For me, a surprise is somewhat like a little flower that all of a sudden opens itself up to the sunlight without any fear of showing to all those around just a little bit more of itself at that particular moment. With these kinds of surprises occurring in our lives once in a while we are able to cast away some of the shadowy boredom that wants to keep us closed off from joyous living. I always want to be generous in providing positive surprises for others and I want to continue to be grateful when truly given a surprise. Life is sure to be much more interesting.

The following day we continued on for two days' voyage in a small motorized canoe, travelling upriver towards San Carlos in Venezuela. We were captained by Jorge, a young Curripaco tribesman, returning with his wife and children from a kind of shopping trip that had taken them to neighboring river towns in Brazil. Since it was flood season in the Amazon at that time, we were not able to pause on the journey very often because there were no easily accessible places to tie up the boat for the time of our bathroom activity needs. The tops of trees whose trunks are submerged many feet underwater are the usual momentary places for such needs but such places are not so readily accessible when one is on this kind of river trip. *Terra firma* just is not available; only treetops are visible. We tended to keep on moving ... for hours and hours! But when Nature calls as one is sequestered within a small canoe loaded with passengers and cargo, and at a time when one least expects, she will not easily wait. "What to do?" one might ask. Oh, but that is another story!

Young Jorge and his family were not very talkative on this journey. But from his place at the motor, however, he was ever alert for danger like submerged tree trunks, rapids, etc. To maintain such a journey totally attentive to all that is happening, not only on board, but in the water and on the distant shore, manifested to me his great stamina. I wondered what his thoughts were as he guided us two strangers up the river. How much does he know about our worlds, so vastly different from his own? How much do we know

On the Rio Negro, Brazil

about his world of rivers and jungle? I had much to ponder as the hours passed by. The warm, moist air blowing against my body, the constantly changing forestscape, and the descending sun and rising moon made for a most introspective time for this part of my *journey's dreaming*. As soon as we arrived the next morning at our river captain's village, we were given the utmost of hospitality according to their customs.

That same day, having passed Cucui, the Rio Negro's last Brazilian armed forces outpost, we arrived at another kind of military checkpoint on the river. It was totally unlike any other that I had ever experienced. As our canoe pulled to shore, I glanced to my right, noticing some individuals with fully automatic weapons disappearing into foxhole-like areas behind the trees. Fear overcame me for a moment, but then it subsided. A few hundred feet from the canoe we could see a dilapidated old cement building with a palm leaf thatched roof. In the middle of its veranda I saw a bed covered with mosquito netting and an official looking person, seemingly not dressed in proper military uniform, sitting in front of it and looking like he was just waking up. He was surrounded by about ten or more men with automatic weapons and the like, each one ready for action. I was not sure if we had entered upon some kind of terrorist camp because the rest of the men with guns were wearing rubber beach sandals, jungle-camouflage shorts, tank-tops, and floppy military hats. Long knives were attached to their sides. Each and every one of them appeared to be in the early twenties, their officer slightly older. All were slender, fighting fit, and, I came to learn later, crack troops of the Venezuelan army.

Venezuelan military checkpoint; I am holding a soldier's pet jungle snake, 2006

Santiago and I approached very slowly, a bit apprehensive, for quite a few rifles were trained on us. I thought to myself, "How easy it would be for us to be killed, our bodies quickly disposed of in this watery jungle, and nobody would ever hear about us again." The officer motioned us forward and we presented our passports and papers. As I looked around I noticed one young soldier near me, gun in hand and ready for anything, with a large snake hanging around his neck, and it was slowly moving. A long, uncomfortable silence ensued, while the officer checked out papers.

All of a sudden, before Santiago offered any words that I thought might be dangerously misunderstood by our hosts, I felt compelled to ask in my best Spanish if I could hold the snake for a while. Surprised by my query, and with all eyes on me, the soldier looked over at his officer who then gave the nod for him to share his mascot with me for a while. It was a strange moment and, I suppose, a bit comical. Right away Santiago told them I was a priest, perhaps hoping that this would somehow help matters. This made for a look of surprise on their faces much greater than before. It also set everybody at ease, but not too much, for all the guns were still trained on us.

After a few moments of small talk and pleasantries, and noticing near me a small shrine with a statue of Our Lady of Mount Carmel, I offered to come back soon to celebrate Mass for them. One can only surmise what these rag-tag soldiers thought at that suggestion. I was even bold enough by now to suggest that they honor her properly by giving the statue a much needed new paint job! And, surprisingly, they agreed. Soon thereafter we left to continue our journey, our papers properly approved. Our Lady of Mount Carmel was the name of my church in Carmel Valley. She, I came to find out after this armed forces moment, is also the patroness of the Venezuelan army. Strange connections, I would say. Why do I often find myself in the midst of such strange connections? I blame it not so much on *the journey* as *the dream.*

Two days later, while at the airport in Puerto Ayacucho, Nancy, Santiago's wife, introduced me to an officer waiting to take a plane. Somehow he either recognized me from some other meeting, or knew of me from others; I am not so sure now. Perhaps he thought that I was one of those American evangelical New Tribes missionaries that recently had been given less than a year to pack up and leave

Venezuela because it was felt that their methods were harmful to Amazon indigenous cultures. He was pleasant as we spoke together, as was his spouse. I was later informed that, unlike many fellow officers who spend a lot of public and private time in this distant and secluded town with their chosen mistresses, this particular soldier of rank is well known and respected for faithfulness to his wife. He enjoys dining in public with her whenever there is an opportunity and is, I believe, a good example for all who behold him. I was also told shortly after the meeting that he was the very same general recently appointed to be responsible for any necessary quick military response to defend the whole Venezuelan Amazon region should it be attacked by the United States!

I feel privileged, honored, and at the same time, humbled that I have been given a few opportunities to experience something of what is actually happening to some tribes and individuals in this part of the rainforest today. Though immense, the Amazon is like a mother continually giving birth and providing for her children. She is also delicate, fragile. Yet the whole world is somehow linked to her life-giving watery ambiance and its inhabitants, especially the human beings dwelling within her forested soil and moist pathways. I number some of these wonderful people as friends now and for the future. Perhaps I can be of some greater service to them as time flows by just like the meandering Rio Negro which gave me a time apart to ponder the vastness of life.

Guyana

I had always wanted to visit Guyana since childhood days. Sheila James was my Guyanese piano teacher and her younger sister, Dallas, my first childhood girlfriend back in London, while their relative, Len, was my Dad's good friend. I remember that he was one of our first neighbors to acquire his own motorcar. This was quite an accomplishment for anyone, even a Commonwealth immigrant, to have a personal car in post-war England. In those days this South American country was known to us as British Guiana, but it achieved its independence in 1966 and began to spell its name somewhat differently: Guyana.

While visiting Brazil in 2004, Santiago and I decided to see what Guyana was really like. We had travelled to Boa Vista, a well-planned 1970's era city situated on the Orinoco River. As it was about two hour's drive away from the border, we decided to hire a taxi to take us in the direction of this English-speaking nation. The isolated border crossing was for me a bit out of the ordinary. It appeared to be a bridgeless river. We hired a canoe for the several hundred-yard crossing and its boatman suggested to me that we could go either to nearby Lethem or downriver a short distance further to Saint Ignatius Mission. I opted for the second choice. At that moment Santiago panicked a bit, probably thinking that we were going to get robbed along the way. So immediately upon getting off at Lethem, we unfortunately discovered that we had over a mile or so to walk to the village crossroads. On this our lengthy stroll we somehow bypassed the immigration and customs office. There was just no easily visible sign for it. On the other hand, we did notice a very officious-looking man staring at us from a distant building shaded by some trees. A passing truck then gave us a ride partway to the mission grounds, but first I had to change my Brazilian money into bona fide Guyanese currency in order to pay for the ride.

The heat was really oppressive as we arrived at the mission after our arduous hike. The housekeeper, quite surprised to see foreign visitors, told us that her priest was arriving very soon on the next plane from Georgetown, the capital, and that it would be good for us to greet him there. So we walked all the way back to Lethem, greeted him, and then traced the road back with him to the mission. The heat was still with us all the time.

Saint Ignatius is a Jesuit mission, and its priest, Oliver Rafferty, was an Irishman who usually taught at Cambridge University, but now was committing himself to serve the mission for five years. I was quite impressed with his work. Here was a celebrated intellectual as well as a fine pastoral missionary in the land of the Wapishana and Makuxi tribes. He offered us typical Irish hospitality, allowing us also to spend some time with his library books. It took me by surprise to find that a good number of the books had been partially eaten by termites. But, luckily, they had spared a number of "Amerindian" books. I took note of some that I thought important enough for my own library at home. Later, I sent a number of spiritual books from

California that I thought might replace some of those destroyed by the humidity and voracious termites, remembering to place them in clear plastic bags for their future preservation.

I felt privileged to celebrate Mass for him while he went out for the day to take care of some surrounding mission stations. During the joyful liturgy I noticed that about half of the folks assembled were shoeless, not because they were in need, but because they would rather more directly feel Mother Earth's presence through their feet. This custom is common for many people, usually when they are at home, but especially for Natives in environments where nature is abundant. The drum and rattle were used for the songs. Afterwards everyone left by the front door, only to gather above the river to say together some special prayers. It was unusual, but a very nice, and obviously local, custom.

We then flew to Georgetown. Beforehand I knew very little about this capital on the south side of the Caribbean. I was really shocked to see blackish brown water being emitted from the taps in what we thought was a fine hotel. The management said that it was normal and safe. But I had my doubts. The heat and humidity were extra oppressive for me, though.

Very soon we located the Walter Roth Museum of Anthropology. The curator, a Native woman named Desray Caesar Fox, took lunch with us and was most helpful in answering my questions about Guyanese tribes. Outside of Guyana, we in the north do not know very much about ""Amerindians" from that part of the Americas. She encouraged us to participate in a traditional "smoke ceremony" at the university, but there was not enough time for us to do so. Luckily for us, she introduced us to some other wonderful folks who owned Lianacane, a factory that makes furniture and other household items from *liana*, a lengthy jungle vine similar to the ones portrayed in the old Tarzan movies. As we were shown around the factory, I pondered how similar, much thinner, *lianas* had been used for millennia to tie together the whole structure of houses made in the jungle. Neither nails nor metal were ever utilized in the process. On the return flight to Lethem, soaring many hundred feet above the jungle, I enjoyed chatting with the Honourable Carolyn Rodriguez, the Minister of Amerindian Affairs. Based on what she shared as well as from conversations with other folks, it seems to me that Amerindians are usually thought of last in this relatively young country where the majority of its inhabitants retain heritages from Africa or India. I look forward to future visits to this unique Anglophile country situated so near others whose populations communicate in Spanish, Portuguese, Dutch, or French more so than the languages spoken here for millennia.

Colombia

While on a river journey in 2004, Santiago and I ventured across from the Venezuelan side of the waters to Colombia, disembarking at Puerto Inírida in the Guianía section of the country. Though we were surrounded by thick jungle in an area known also more recently for its terrorism and kidnappings, I was intrigued nonetheless to go there. I remember that on our journey upriver one woman in our boat was clutching the largest chicken that I ever saw sequestered in a net bag! It was quite a sight to see her go up to the customs checkpoint with all of her luggage and a squirming monster chicken as well. While waiting my turn, I became terribly horrified upon noticing hundreds of large black spiders with extra-long pointy legs hanging from the roof of the *muelle* (wharf). I thought that at any moment they would descend upon us. But, as it was early in the day, perhaps they were just resting! Santiago suggested that we head for the local Catholic church to seek hospitality because he had heard already about its pastor, Padre Caliche (Carlos Enrique Ortíz Romero).

We were in for quite a surprise as we were welcomed by the smile of a young bearded priest whose long black hair fell in curly rings all around his head. He looked as if he belonged in some ancient renaissance painting rather than in an off-the-river jungle village setting. As we were to discover among the locals, he was both quite popular and an artist as well. His church sanctuary displayed a large, over-the-altar mural portraying a strong, youthful yet powerful Christ (who, curiously, looked a bit like the priest himself!). At lunch he sadly and in measured speech shared with us that just recently some terrorists had sent a bomb-filled, banana-laden canoe downriver towards the town in order to blow up its local military base. An innocent woman was killed in the explosion. He became quite animated in telling us these things, and from this short encounter, I could see that he is one of those priests who from time immemorial , and not unlike me, seem to prefer to exist on the cutting edge of life.

As it appears to me, contemporary Colombian city culture is rapidly overrunning the ancient domain of a not quite so frenzied jungle. The Guianía area that we were visiting comprises the ancestral lands of the Curripaco, Puinave, and Piapoco tribes, who make up over fifty percent of the present population. New people from other places in the country arrive each day in great numbers, seeking a new life. Some are escaping the narco-traffickers and paramilitary groups and other gangs who control vast sections of Colombia.

At the confluence of the Inírida and Guaviare Rivers, surprisingly Puerto Inírida boasts a beautiful new library. Though the books it contains are few, the people are proud of the facility. Cement paths embroidered by lush flowers and other native plants leading up to the building are still in development, yet its nearby roads are not quite finished. The government must be behind much of the investment in this isolated area. Perhaps it is to become a model city for the future of the country. Who really knows?

Most of the vehicles in this city are small and three-wheeled. Yet signs of rapid growth are everywhere. I hope that the town planners take many things into account so that past planning mistakes that have occurred in other cities do not repeat themselves here and in similar places throughout the country. For me, this bustling town had a very different "feel" from nearby places like San Fernando de Atabapo, a town which in a like manner is situated in Venezuela across and downriver about thirty miles.

Padre Caliche, jungle missionary, Puerto Inírida, Guianían Amazon, Colombia

More Recently

OVER THE YEARS I have adopted the words of Dag Hammerskold, a former Secretary of the United Nations, as my personal motto: "For all that has been: Thanks. To all that will be: Yes." Even at this point in my life's *journey,* with more than thirty-five years of being a priest, I look forward each day to meeting many new people and being involved with any new situations that God unfolds for me. I do this as a believer in Jesus and with the openness of his Spirit for all people of good will. *The dream* keeps me going.

Let me mention a few of the things that have happened lately in my life.

Catholic Digest Magazine

In March of 2000 a perennial national magazine, *Catholic Digest,* published an article on my life entitled: "Conversation with a Culture-hopping Priest." I was quite pleased with it because it helped to affirm and validate what many priests, sisters, lay missionaries, as well as folks of other Christian churches on this continent have been trying to do for over 500 years: share the Good News. Often making mistakes of judgment along the way, they invariably took the time to exchange their share of the divine goodness that exists in each culture and sought to let it be shared inter-generationally. This magazine article apparently gave my life's work some country-wide exposure and I was quite pleased with some of the correspondence that came from it. Others folks, quite unknown to me before, seemed to understand my work and wanted to confirm it in some way or even help with it. It was a good feeling to have.

Praying at Wailing Wall, Jerusalem, 1998

Visiting grave of Farm Workers' Union founder and popular saint, César Chavez, Keane, California

Nowadays lots of folks seem to be fascinated with attempts to reconcile different spiritual paths. I do not believe that it is really that difficult to do. But in the great flux of life it may take some time to accomplish. We are all related to each other, and every being that exists does so because of our common origin in the One who we commonly call God. We are all sustained on a daily basis by that same Creative Being, and are all brought into a good future by the very same Fulfiller of all Life.

I am pleased that I have had the opportunity to visit the Holy Land (Israel/Palestine), meet many people there, and pray for peace in our troubled world. Whenever possible I take myself to more local places for prayer, especially if they are surrounded by nature or are significantly unique because of the individuals who lived or died there. I especially feel close to the United Farm Workers' Union organizer, César Chavez, who many times set foot within our Diocese of Monterey to help our people.

Soon after this article, people from the national radio show, *The Osgood File,* contacted me for an interview. Once again I felt like *the journey* was continuing, but in a more public way, perhaps fulfilling for me a heretofore unknown part of the *dream*. They sent someone out to Montana to tape me singing a native healing song as I celebrated the sacrament of the sick with my adopted Dad Irvin at the family's campsite during Crow Fair. Though at the time he was very sick, nevertheless he expressed a deep and abiding faith in Creator's healing power as it is distributed among many earthly spiritual helpers, his adopted son included. I could sense that he was really proud of me and encouraged me to continue in my sacred work.

A number of times I have been invited by members of the Native American Church to come to one of their all-night ceremonies that are usually held on the occasion of a special life-change event like a life-threatening illness, the death of a loved one, or even graduation from a school or university. One special peyote ceremony took place near Caguas, Puerto Rico. At that year's Encounter about nine of us from near where I live in Monterey County were able to participate. Our youth even put up the teepee (traditional dwelling of the plains Peoples that is preferred for this kind of ceremony) and, since this is no small feat for the unpracticed, we were especially glad they were properly acknowledged by the leaders of the ceremony.

The ritual involves an all-night ceremony during which participants optionally ingest peyote buttons or a tea made from them. A special drum containing water is utilized. The water inside it allows for a great variety of sound tones to be heard throughout the night's sacred songs. Many participants shake beautiful fans made from macaw parrot feathers and others keep time with the drum with their rattles as fast-paced songs of praise are sung. At a certain moment the roadman, the leader, allows the medicine to be distributed. As it is a sacramental action for the participants, everyone who desires so takes a little. More songs lead into a time of intense prayer. I found myself, along with some others, actually praying out loud on my knees for all my parishioners and loved ones for about forty-five minutes, even though I was not thinking in terms of clock time. Everyone felt truly blessed when cool, clear, refreshing blessed water was brought for us to drink in the morning.

It is difficult to sit for about twelve hours in the same place, and yet this is part of the prayer "sacrifice," I suppose. Short homilies, helpful little sermons about living in a good way, are an integral part of this healing ceremony. There is nothing for anyone to fear because the spiritual leader as a true presider is always watchful. What happens to the participants during the ceremony? Well, they offer prayer and are prayed for by others present, and healing occurs on a variety of levels. The essentials of the peyote ceremony are ancient, going back even before the time of the Aztec and Huichol Peoples of Mexico, I am sure. Nowadays it is slowly spreading out to both Native and non-Natives, often being celebrated in Spanish or in a hybrid of languages. It must be said that many pre-Colombian forms of similar ceremonies utilizing the plants that Creator gave us remain part of the heritage of the Peoples throughout the Americas even today.

An Ocean View: Third Pastorate: Seaside

My most recent parish assignment has been to Saint Francis Xavier Church in Seaside, near Monterey, California. Throughout over half a century of history, this faith community has been known to be multilingual and multicultural in scope. It is definitely a place of learning for anyone who happens to be assigned there. Parishioners include African Americans, Filipinos, Tongans, Hawaiians, Germans, Italians, Bolivians, Guamanians, Mexicans, and a variety of Central and South Americans, and people from a whole host of other cultural groups. Native Americans must also be included among them, though they number in the minority. Still, I have always tried to

Some of my Tongan parishioners, St. Francis Xavier Church, Seaside, California, 2007

At a Native youth mass in Carmel Valley Mountains, 2007

reach out to them in friendship and service. Chumash, Ohlone, and Esselen People live nearby, but upon occasion I have come into contact with Choctaws, Cherokees, Lakotas, and Navajos, and representatives of other tribes. It is a great pity that in California the general population does not know very much about its fellow citizens of Native heritage. Other than hearing about the ubiquitous casinos, the Native presence is not usually acknowledged by a lot of folks.

Ohlone Leader Patrick Orozco, Felton, California, 2008

Ohlone dancers, Felton, California, 2008

Activities

At times on *the journey* I have been called upon to accomplish some things that were not in actual fact revealed to me through my own received religious or cultural heritage, but rather that came in *the dreams* or longings of other folks. Over the years, I have been called upon to do *limpias* (cleansing blessings) that are always Christ-centered, but which often express traditions of the Andean Peoples or of those from Central America. Both traditional Catholic religious symbolic items as well as native "medicine" objects are utilized in these special activities that really have to do with cleansing and blessing. Seaside and its environs contain a large population of folks from Oaxaca in southern Mexico. Most are familiar with the tradition of *limpias* as are many other culturally diverse persons.

I can remember a time right after a Sunday Spanish Mass when I was called upon to visit a sick young woman. She had been sent home from the hospital because they did not really know how to treat her. As I entered the apartment, I noticed clouds of copal incense filling the rooms. I knew right away that this would call for a more indigenous expression of the sacrament that I was about to celebrate with her. She was listless in her bed. As the concerned relatives and friends gathered closer around her, I gently spoke to her in Spanish in my best comforting voice. The room was really full. I laid my hands on her head and anointed her with sacred oil and gave her communion. I then called for more copal and blessed her with its sacred smoke. A drum was handed to me and I sang an Indian song that I knew. She gradually opened her eyes, smiled, and began to talk in a normal way. I left shortly. The next day I was told that she had fully recovered. I was pleased.

Another time after a Sunday Spanish mass I was handed a little child who had very little control of its motor movements. The eyes could not focus on one object for very long and would keep moving from side to side. I caressed the little one and felt urged to sing a native style lullaby-like melody. The parents looked on as I sang very softly, but just loud enough for the child. Gradually its precious little wandering eyes were turned to me and remained fixed on my face. I then realized that part of the cure for this new-to-our-world creation of God was a mother or father's lullaby. Such an ancient child-raising practice does not seem to be so proficiently practiced nowadays as our vain attempts to always speak of things only in realistic, technological, or even practical, terminology have taken precedence. We have a great need to regain past wisdom, I believe, for it will aid us much in our future together. Happily, the parents followed my advice and I have observed since remarkable improvement in the child.

Sometimes Aztec dancers, or *matachines* (mummer-like religious dancers blending Spanish and Indian traditions from New Mexico and northern Mexico), came to help us often in special liturgies throughout the year. During these celebrations I might use church incense in a more indigenous way, like blessing the bread or the wine in the form of a cross over a pot of burning copal or sage or cedar, depending on who was present to appreciate the ritual. I would never impose such ways on anyone; only when I knew that it was the right thing to do for the folks present. Often a parishioner would comment that I was helping to bring out "Indianness" in Mexican or more south of the border folks longing for this kind of acculturation in church ceremonies.

I believe that there is a great hunger among the People for this kind of activity that utilizes tribal ways for expressing both personal and communal faith. Faith is always much deeper than any doctrinal or dogmatic words, important though they are to identify the mysterious presence of Creator among us in the unique Son who is cherished from the heart of the Maker of all. Faith is also expressed in something much prior to words, and that is in culture. Spiritual heritage rides on it like a horse carries its rider. Our present and future priests, ministers, and other spiritual leaders need to be aware of this, I would dare to say. Knowing and respecting just a few of these ancient traditions will be most helpful for any upcoming leaders, no matter what is one's own cultural background. I am passionately committed to continue to encourage this kind of acculturation. Over the last few years in my area we have experienced a great influx of people from Oaxaca, southern Mexico. Some are Zapotecs, having Spanish as a second language and now English as a third. I am pleased to report that one of our diocesan priests, Father Greg Sandman, plans to learn Zapotec or another Oaxacan language in order to be of greater help in the future to these newcomers.

Happily, our new bishop, Richard García, also of Mexican heritage, is most interested in Native concerns within the Diocese of Monterey. He has made me his personal liaison to local tribes in order to assist whenever their certain issues require our spiritual expertise, especially issues connected with five California missions located within our diocesan boundaries. Several times I have been asked by the Salinan Tribe to celebrate special masses at Missions San Antonio and San Miguel. These masses remember all the saints and faithful departed on their feast days. The liturgy always has Salinan language and ceremony components. Processions after the masses

With Bishop Richard García and Navajo friend Roderick Thomas, 2007

Celebrating Mass with Salinan Tribe at San Antonio Mission, California, with Fathers Ray Tintle, Larry Gosselin, and Dennis Peterson, 2009

lead to the cemeteries where native way prayers for the ancestors and the more recently departed are offered along with tobacco and sage. A key player in all of this is John Warren with his New World Orchestra. These multicultural musicians of different ages, not only offer contemporary spiritual music, but they excel in bringing back into the liturgy both Native and Mission-period Latin music that a hundred or so years ago was such a usual part of the People's spiritual life along with their own more ancient ceremonies.

At the present time I have taken a much needed break from the ever-increasing busy-ness of parish life in order to serve as a Catholic chaplain at a large hospital in Monterey. The pastoral team approach allows us as members of world faiths to minister, to serve, the needs of a variety of patients who reflect the cultural and ethnic pluralism and varieties of religious experience that are so abundant in California. I have also the opportunity to help out my brother priests in nearby parishes with all the important liturgical services. Being free of a certain amount of heavy administrative responsibility for a short while is a real treat for me nowadays and I really like it, but the parish is my real home.

Future Possibilities

People Circles

The circle is a wonderful symbol because it is so inclusive. It can grow or diminish itself, whatever the circumstances around it or within it. Circles do not have to be only static, lacking movement; they can also express activity, as in a living cell. Some move clockwise, others in an opposite direction. Perhaps some just vibrate with energy.

Beginning with my own circle of friends, as time goes by I would like to see active circles, dynamic wheels of creative action, put to the service of peace and justice, expressing in concrete actions the words of a bygone spiritual leader, Pope Paul VI, who suggested: "If you want peace, work for justice." As circles move about the planes of our human existence, we have wonderful opportunities to observe "what is really going on," to reflect on what should be done, allowing for some appropriate decision making, and then we can wheel ourselves into action.

As we ourselves move about, some of our circles may already be seeking or sharing wisdom from generations past. Native folks would know what I mean here by this. No matter what is our received culture, that human ambiance in which we try to live well, our traditions need to be constantly renewed in each generation so that they might be rolled forward to the next one: intact, freshened up a bit, but intact nonetheless. Ways of meditation and prayers, songs, dances, traditional clothing styles, foods, tattoos, hair styles, body painting, special ways of oratory, even unique educational methods: all of these can be taught and practiced within a circle of any dimension: a family, band, clan, or tribe, a church or religious group, a nation, or even a gathering of nations. Boards, committees, schools, parliaments, congresses, and other forms of purposeful human gathering all have their places. More often than not the "we—they" syndrome is built right into their *modus operandi*. Perhaps this is inescapable. But there are other models as well, the circle being one that is tried and true; and, from my own experience and point of view, it is a good posture for worship.

Native Island Youth Cultural Exchanges

I recently attended the X Native Gathering of the Americas in Puerto Rico. A few of us were attendees at the first one, but I did notice many new faces among us this time. A good number of folks from the Dominican Republic were with us this time, most of them

Juan Trejo and I with Nobel Peace Prize winner Rigoberta Menchú Tum from Guatemala in Caguas, Puerto Rico, 2008

With Bishop of Caguas and brother of Rigoberta Menchú Tum at Native Gathering of the Americas ceremony, Caguas, Puerto Rico, 2008

being youths. They expressed a lot of the ancient Taino heritage in their dances and songs, but it seemed as if they thought that the Tainos were a past reality of people now very much extinct. As the days passed they appeared to relate well to the Puerto Rican Taino youth who each day live their heritage in robust ways. These kids became a mirror for the Dominicans of what it means to be a contemporary person of Taino heritage.

I have had an idea brewing within me for some time and it has to do with a Caribbean youth cultural interchange. In speaking to various leaders about it, I believe that it just might be feasible. It concerns young Tainos (Arawak heritage) from both Puerto Rico and the Dominican Republic getting together for a period of time with Kalinago (Carib heritage) youth from the tiny island of Dominica to learn more about, to further, their cultural and spiritual knowledge. Dugout canoe building, basketry, traditional cooking, language, song and dance, crafts, all of this and more should become available to the youth of each and every island where there is an indigenous presence, no matter how small it may be. As time goes by, other indigenous communities might be added to the list, perhaps

Nahuatl-speaking friend Felipe Vargas between two Lakota friends, traditional Chief Dwayne Goodface and actor Lee Plentywolf, Native Gathering of the Americas, Caguana Ceremonial Park, Utuado, Puerto Rico, 2008

At University of Cayey, Puerto Rico, during 10th Native Gathering of the Americas, 2008

Cuban Tainos as well, so that the exchange becomes ongoing and productive. Even Chumash youth, and those of other California tribes that have an ocean-going heritage, would benefit from such an exchange and be able to promote something similar on California coastal waters that would eventually bring in others living within the Oregon-to-Alaska Pacific rim. I would like to be part of such a potentially historic cultural interchange. It can only lead to further good, I believe.

Indigenous Journeys in the Four Directions

Over the years I have become familiar with various aspects of indigenous worship through study and participation in different kinds of ceremonies. More recently, I recommended to some international tribal leaders that a kind of indigenous passage or sacred run, or pilgrimage, should be designed and implemented among the people of a particular island (like Borikén, that is, Puerto Rico) or a country (like Panama) or even a larger area (like Mesoamerica) which includes several nations.

At a Taino celebration, Puerto Rico

We California delegates share gifts of cedar prayer offerings with Tainos at Native Gathering of the Americas, Caguana Ceremonial Park, Utuado, Puerto Rico, 2008

I had been thinking of a journey composed of runners, walkers, or even those who could travel by bicycle or automobile. In each area, large or small, each one of the sacred directions of east, south, west and north would be delineated so as to provide routes of travel for the participants. Each directional base would be centered on an already-existing site sacred to the people, like a rock formation, a waterfall, an ancient village or ceremonial place. Or other contemporary places, like a park or a tower, might be chosen as long as they become representative of the cardinal directions. At each of these sacred points ceremonies would be celebrated, the participants being blessed by their own spiritual leaders. Then the task of running, walking, or travelling by other means to a sacred site in the middle of these designated directional points would begin. Journey participants could be tracked by phone and airplane, the progress reported to faraway folks through the media. When all arrive at the central destination point, each and every one of the participants would be joyfully, proudly received before ceremonies and feasting would take place.

I believe that this kind of activity, annual or biennial, would do much to animate the tribes involved as well as provide new vigor and hope to those who claim some quantity of Native heritage. Perhaps this kind of activity could also initiate, conclude, or at least enhance, some type of Indigenous Olympics.

Spiritual Leadership

As an observer, I sometimes find Native People who seem to prefer to be at odds with each other much more than to try to work together in promoting harmony, especially in the context of dealing with the dominant society's often conflicting value systems. The ones who really seem to suffer in these sad affairs are the next generations. Sometimes difficulties are about deciding who really belongs in the tribe, band or local group. Sometimes it is about land or property issues. Often it concerns how much "Indian" someone is by their blood quantum or shade of skin. There might be other issues as well. I would simply like to comment that it is always a good thing to seek the higher ground on these issues, to see the larger view, to realize that when all things are considered, "the honor of

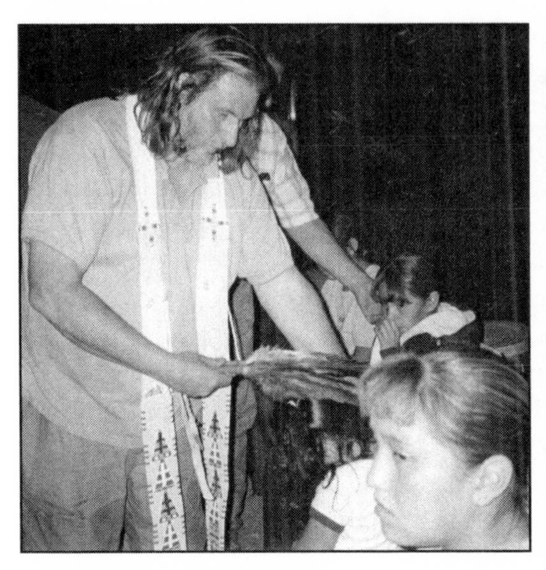

A blessing ceremony, Crow Reservation, Montana, 2004

Sharing with a Piaroa Tribal Congress on Samariapo River, Amazon, Venezuela, 2002

one is indeed the honor of all." This is when a spiritual leader (Native or non-Native, depending on the circumstances) may be helpful for everyone. Everyone's future depends on positive lived-out spirituality which issues forth from the past while still maintaining its relevance in the present moment. What I say here can be translated into the life of any other culture that exists in our modern world.

With our delegates for Native Gathering of the Americas, Tibes, Puerto Rico, 2005

Chumash medicine woman, Adelina Alva-Padilla, with brothers, Carlos and Juan Herrera, champion Tarahumara runners, Chumash Powwow near Santa Barbara, California, 2008

I feel a certain amount of pain for people of all cultures who are marginalized, who are often left out, forgotten, but especially this continent's indigenous Peoples. For us, Native American history is always local history. It is a part of the land forever. But often our educational systems, governmental institutions, or our business enterprises do not always allow for the respect due the faraway past or the near present. I am speaking about the need for other people, newcomers, immigrants, descendants of immigrants, to know of the historical presence and present moment of Native People. Schools are often lacking in this. More Native People need to be invited to classrooms to share moments of their heritage with students of all ages. In turn, these young people will be able to reflect on their own heritages as well. I call this "the mirror effect."

I foresee the future of all people on this planet Earth as being necessarily interconnected in thousands of ways. One way is through personal and communal spirituality. I have found Indigenous People to be very open-minded about things which pertain to religion or spirituality. Like anyone else, they receive gifts and make them personal. Usually they offer gifts in return, often of greater value than the ones received. For over 500 years, even though many mistakes have been made on all sides, a lot of gift-giving, a lot of spiritual sharing, has already happened and everyone has been affected by it. Perhaps now is a good time for those of us in the dominant society, especially including religious people, to become truly open-minded and open-hearted to the ancient heritage of spiritual gifts offered by this hemisphere's tribal Peoples. Ecumenical and inter-religious sharing is a must in this matter. For instance, think of the circle; our church edifices and temples would probably take on a whole new architectural look if we utilized the circle shape much more than the square or oblong! All of us would benefit in some way, I am sure.

I spoke earlier of the evangelical-versus-Catholic syndrome that, sadly, I have seen taking place for the past many years throughout Latin America as well as up here in the North. I know that it is based on ignorance and past prejudices among churches and individuals. But, as some of us in the "religious business" may know, this is just not helpful for anyone, especially Native Peoples. In fact, it has been devastating to both culture and spirituality, as we have come to learn over the last 500 years. Many of us, both individuals and churches, have come to realize this now: that in the past there were lots of good intentions accompanied by a plethora of mistakes. Movies like *At Play in the Fields of the Lord* speak to some of this difficulty. But there are others, and lots of books on the subject as well.

We human beings find that when there is a problem, it is good to sit down together and start communicating about it, to express how it is affecting us. The way then lies open for us to seek paths of understanding and peace together. Good conclusions can be drawn up together. To paraphrase someone else's words: "look, think, consider," and then "act"... but together.

With Episcopal Presiding Bishop, Most Reverend Katherine Jefferts Schori at Saratoga, California, 2008

Visiting Islamic mosque and Maronite Catholic Church across from each other on the same street, Caracas, Venezuela

After a wedding

If I may be so bold, I would like to suggest that for believers in Jesus, no matter their church, denomination, affiliation, race, or culture, a year-long world-level summit regarding various interpretations of Scripture in each of our traditions might be most helpful for all of us. From top world church leaders on down to the local believer in a city or jungle setting, I really believe that it would be beneficial if people took the time to actually listen to each other regarding their received or personal understanding of the Bible. Misinterpretation of Bible passages, words taken out of context and then improperly applied, has done so much damage already and continues to do so in people's lives. In fact, I am passionate about this and, on some of my travels in Latin America, I have tried to promote the idea of such a summit conference. It would definitely take a lot of planning and organization. Many key leaders would have to get on board as this *journey*, guided by the *dream* carrying within itself such potentiality, leads us to "God knows where." The "where" would have to be a good place, for it would be the all-embracing abode of God.

But I am just one person thinking like this here and now. I am sure that there are many others of like mind who appreciate our past religious heritages and want to find good ways to pass them on to future generations, but in ways that are not divisive, that do not rob people of those things in their individual and common lives that

Piaroa Shaman Bolivar and family members, Alta Carinagua, Amazon, Venezuela, 2009

Hiwi Shaman Miguel Gaitan and family, Coromoto, Amazon, Venezuela, 2009

make for good spirituality. Other world religions, like Islam and Buddhism could do likewise, building similar dialogs within themselves as a communal religion, as well as with sisters and brothers in other world faiths, for we are all daughters and sons of our same Creator. It is about giving gifts to one other and knowing the best way, even the best time to give those gifts; and gifts that are free and with no strings attached.

Shaman Raimundo and son preparing ritual sacred drink

In ceremony with Dessano Shaman Raimundo, Tupé, Amazon, Brazil, 2009

Children's first communion mass, Our Lady of Mount Carmel, Carmel Valley, California

A Theology of Ecology

As a Catholic Christian I would like to see my Church take seriously a challenge to continually acculturate, not only our worship, but also our theology so as to express a much deeper indigenous cosmovision. A more balanced understanding of our role as stewards, not dominators, of planetary care should be part of the official proclamation of the Good News for all people to hear. This kind of vision would help everyone to regain much of what has been lost in our society since the onslaught of the industrial revolution and, more recently, the technological revolution. Perhaps many of us need to re-learn how to relate better to Mother Earth, to recognize her as a living being and not just as an object to be dominated. Some "signs of the times" like global warming, and the innumerable varieties of human-caused pollution urge us to reconsider our right relationship with Mother Earth, for I believe that in taking care of her and each other we offer true worship

At my 35th Anniversary of Ordination Mass, Carmel Valley, 2009

House blessing, Salinas, California

to Creator. Such an indigenous "theology of ecology," well studied, would serve us well in years to come. Ah, but it is good to *dream*...

As I continue my *journey* towards the future, my *dreams* ready to be shared with numerous people of good will, and in particular, Indigenous People of good will, may I close for now by paraphrasing an ancient prayer:

May God, who has begun a great work in us, bring it to fulfillment!

Ahóo, Amen!

Where will the next journey lead me?

About the Author

CORNELIUS IAN (SCOTT) MCCARTHY is a priest of the Diocese of Monterey in California. Having spent much time with Native American communities and individuals while living and travelling throughout the Americas, he has come to recognize that the well-being of all people depends upon our proper relation to the creation, our Mother Earth. He holds two Masters Degrees as well as a Doctorate of Ministry, combining these intellectual enterprises with his own experience among many cultures. Recognizing our modern world's difficulties with its use of cutting-edge technology combined with outmoded ways of governance, he seeks to promote the general well-being of all people by teaching the time-honored relationship between worship and personal spirituality. He now focuses his sacred work on encouraging women, men, youth, and children to take glimpses into both past and present cultures so as to visualize a better future for everyone and everything.

CPSIA information can be obtained at www.ICGtesting.com
Printed in the USA
LVOW090459290911

248386LV00002B/49/P